Ultimate TELEVISION SHOWSTOPPERS

Project Managers: Carol Cuellar, Zobeida Pérez, and Donna Salzburg
Art Design: Ken Rehm
Text By: Fucini Productions, Inc.
Special thanks to David, Larry, Gail, Vincent, Mike, and Ken for their creative input

C000194386

CONTENTS

Ultimate TELEVISION SHOWSTOPPERS

Introduction

On August 25, 1900, a scientist named Constantin Perskyi presented a paper to the International Electricity Congress in Paris that described an electro-magnetic process for transmitting visual images. He gave his report an unusual one-word title—"Television."

Perskyi wasn't the only researcher in the early 1900s working on ways to use the power of electricity to send pictures from one point to another. In fact, his ideas would have little or no bearing on the ultimate development of this new technology. But his term "television" quickly caught on. His contemporaries soon stopped coming up with clumsy names like "telephot" and "telectroscope" to describe their work and began using Perskyi's more catchy phrase.

Within two or three generations, "television" would become one of the world's first truly universal words. Go to any village in any country on any continent and mention "television," and people will understand exactly what you mean.

Everyone everywhere knows television because it has touched our lives in so many different ways: as a form of entertainment, an educational tool, a source of news—as the ultimate connection to the world outside our door. Television is the contemporary world's campfire, the place around which we gather at the end of the day to share stories, relive events, celebrate triumphs, and try to make sense of our tragedies.

Television has given our daily news a sense of intimacy and immediacy that would have been unimaginable in an earlier era. Through the power of television, people around the world can, for the first time in history, share the same vivid images of events as they unfold—from great celebrations like the opening ceremonies of the Olympics to painful tragedies like the terrorist attack on the World Trade Center.

It is only fitting that music, the universal language, should play an important role in television, the first true universal medium. From the earliest days of TV in the late 1940s and early 1950s, directors have skillfully employed music to establish the right mood for their programming, adding a sense of excitement to action dramas, a chilling fear to horror shows, and a light-hearted warmth to comedies. Even quiz show producers have recognized the value of music. Think of how the familiar "Jeopardy Theme," with its tick-tocking back-and-forth melody, fills our TV room with nail-biting suspense when a contestant strives to arrive at the correct question.

Songs That Set the Mood

In some respects, music has played an even more important role in television than it has in film. (That's saying a lot since the film industry has shown how highly it regards music by creating Academy Awards for Best Song and Best Score.) Working on the small screen, TV directors don't have the same opportunities enjoyed by filmmakers to use breathtaking scenery or dazzling special effects to create the right mood.

This was especially true in the early days of television, when the available technology was less advanced and most shows were in black and white, while movies were in color.

As a result of these limitations, the makers of television programs became very adept at using music to create a rich and deeply textured background for their programming. Quite often, a TV director would set the

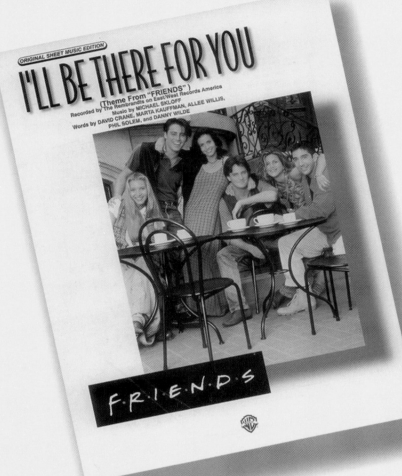

stage for the mood of a drama or comedy by having an evocative theme song play at the start of the show. This tradition, which began in the 1950s with songs like the "Peter Gunn Theme," was still going strong when the new century arrived, as evidenced by "I'll Be There for You," the theme from the hit program "Friends." Written by Henry Mancini, the cool, jazzy "Peter Gunn Theme" became a No. 1 *Billboard* hit in 1959. For Mancini, a legend who would eventually be nominated for an incredible 72 Grammy Awards, "Peter Gunn" marked the beginning of a long creative relationship with director Blake Edwards, a partnership that would span 26 hit films.

Music is versatile—it effectively sets the mood for a drama as well as a comedy. Just ask the millions of fans who tune in every week to the Emmy Award-winning

program "Friends." The breezy and free-flowing theme song "I'll Be There for You" captures the spirit of "Friends" and contributes to the upbeat mood of this comedy about independent young people living in New York City. On another level, the song can also be appreciated as a tribute to the kind of loyal friendships that are portrayed in this hit comedy.

Written and recorded by the Rembrandts—the duo of Phil Solem and Danny Wilde—"I'll Be There for You" became a hit in its own right apart from its association with the hit TV program. The song reached Top Twenty *Billboard* status in 1995 and reached the top of the *Billboard* Airplay Chart.

Songs That Set a Standard

Like the "Peter Gunn Theme" and "I'll Be There for You," quite a few TV tunes have become major hits on the *Billboard* charts, including "Hawaii Five-O," "Bad Boys" from "Cops," and "The Rockford Files Theme." Some theme songs have even had a broad influence on musical trends that extended far beyond television. Such was the case with two of the top TV songs from the 1980s, the "Miami Vice Theme" and "The Hill Street Blues Theme."

In 1985, the "Miami Vice Theme" became a No. 1 *Billboard* hit and earned two Grammy Awards for its composer, Jan Hammer. A Czech-born multi-instrumentalist, Hammer captured the pulse of the "Miami Vice" detective drama with a unique piece of music that offered a smooth blend of sophisticated sounds. Hammer's composition not only provided a perfect background for the actions of detectives James "Sonny" Crockett and Ricardo Tubbs, but it also

helped draw attention to the emerging Miami Latin musical style that groups like Gloria Estefan and the Miami Sound Machine were introducing to mainstream audiences in the 1980s.

Another popular detective show of the 1980s, "Hill Street Blues," also produced an influential theme song. The elegant yet simple piano solos of "The Hill Street Blues Theme" defined a new urbane style for pop and TV music composers. Written by Mike Post and Larry Carlton, the theme song won two Grammy Awards in 1981 for Best Instrumental Composition and Best Pop Instrumental Performance.

Songs That Tell a Story

Throughout the history of television, theme songs have often served another important function—they've "set the stage" by providing viewers with background material about a program at the beginning of every episode. Back in the 1960s, first-time viewers might not have been familiar with the story line of "Gilligan's Island," but after listening to the show's theme song, "The Ballad of Gilligan's Isle," they knew all about the *Minnow* and its fateful trip.

Narrative theme songs like "The Ballad of Gilligan's Isle" entertained viewers as they told the story of the show. In so doing, they saved that most precious of TV commodities—time. By running a theme song at the start of each episode, the makers of a TV program didn't have to slow down their plot to include background material.

In the case of "Gilligan's Island," the show's theme song also provided a shortcut to getting the series started. Since the song explained who all the characters were and how they got on the "uncharted desert isle," there was no need for the program's producers to make an episode that showed the wreck of the *Minnow*. Gilligan, the Skipper, and the other castaways were already stranded on their island when the first episode began, but this didn't matter because the entire history of the shipwreck was covered in the theme song.

Other background songs, like "(Meet) The Flintstones," served to introduce a TV program's unusual characters. Written by Californian Hoyt Curtin, the theme for the cartoon "The Flintstones" is one of the most frequently played pieces of music on television. The song not only told us about this "modern Stone Age family," but it also helped popularize such phrases as "yabba, dabba doo." In addition to

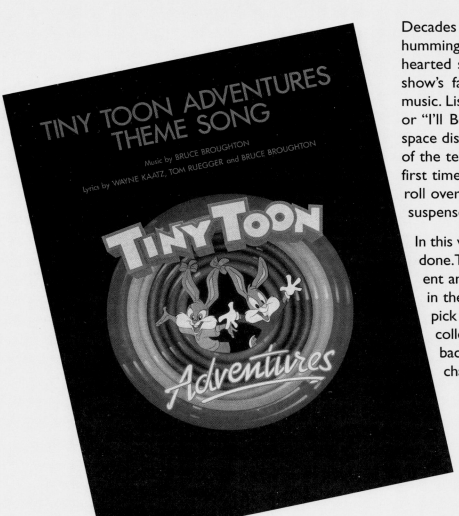

TINY TOON ADVENTURES
THEME SONG

Music by BRUCE BROUGHTON

Lyrics by WAYNE KAATZ, TOM RUEGGER and BRUCE BROUGHTON

TINY TOON
Adventures

Decades after "Mr. Ed" ended its prime-time run, humming a few bars of Livingston and Evans' light-hearted song still brings a smile to the faces of the show's fans. That's part of the magic of television music. Listening to TV songs like the "Mr. Ed Theme" or "I'll Be There for You" seems to make time and space disappear. Suddenly, there we are again in front of the television, watching our favorite show for the first time and being amazed by its ability to make us roll over laughing or sit at the edge of our couch in suspense.

In this way, TV songs do what good music has always done. They open a direct passage between our present and our past, our brains and our hearts—and, in the process, they enrich our lives. So go ahead, pick up that remote control and surf through this collection of television music. It's sure to bring back memories of the great shows and colorful characters you loved to watch.

"(Meet) The Flintstones," Curtin penned memorable songs for cartoon shows like "Huckleberry Hound," "The Jetsons," and "Yogi Bear."

Some TV themes not only introduced us to a show's characters, but they also had the star perform in them. This was the case with the "Mr. Ed Theme," which was written by Jay Livingston and Ray Evans. Before turning their attention to TV's amazing talking horse, this talented team had collaborated on three Academy Award-winning songs: "Buttons and Bows," "Mona Lisa," and "Que Será, Será (Whatever Will Be, Will Be)."

Livingston and Evans' "Mr. Ed Theme" featured well-crafted lyrics and a catchy melody, which has made it an all-time sing-along favorite. But the highlight of this music for many TV viewers was hearing Mr. Ed talk at the beginning and end of the song. Listening to Mr. Ed against the background of his theme song set the tone for this wonderfully offbeat comedy about one of the most unusual "pets" in the history of television.

TV Trivia

1. The original name of "The Flintstones" was "The Flagstones." The show's famous theme song "(Meet) The Flintstones" wasn't introduced until its third season.

2. Neal Hefti, who composed "The Batman Theme," was an accomplished jazz musician who worked with Woody Herman, Harry James, and Count Basie.

3. Merv Griffin created the game show "Jeopardy!" in 1964 in his apartment. Griffin also composed the show's theme song. "Jeopardy!" and "Wheel of Fortune" were the first TV shows to become Olympic sponsors.

4. "The Fugitive" TV series was based on the real-life case of Dr. Sam Sheppard.

5. In 1947, there were only 60,000 TV sets in the entire U.S., about 66 percent of them in New York City. In 1952, the number of TV sets in use reached 20 million.

6. In 1959, the prime-time schedules of the major networks included 32 westerns.

7. Fred Gwynne, who played Herman Munster on "The Munsters," was a Harvard graduate and Shakespearean actor.

8. "Batman" was so popular at one point in the 1960s that it ran twice a week.

9. According to Nielsen Media Research, the average U.S. household watched seven hours eleven minutes of television a day in 1997, just six minutes more than the average a decade earlier.

10. "The Andy Griffith Show," which ran from 1960 to 1968, finished No. 4 in the Nielsen ratings its first year, No. 1 its last year, and never fell below No. 7 in between.

11. When U.S. Senator and former astronaut John Glenn was launched into space for the second time (October 29, 1998), it became the first news event to be broadcast commercially on High Definition Television.

12. More than 25 million people tuned in to the final 1997 episode of "Mad About You" to witness the birth of Jamie and Paul's baby.

13. "Friends" star Jennifer Aniston's father is John Aniston, who starred in the daytime soap opera "Days of Our Lives." Her godfather was Telly Savalas of "Kojak" fame.

14. Della Reese, star of the hit "Touched by an Angel" does indeed have a heavenly heritage. The multi-talented actress began her professional career at the age of 13 touring with the great gospel singer Mahalia Jackson. At 18, she formed the Meditation Singers and became the first artist to bring gospel music to the casinos of Las Vegas. Reese was a guest on "The Ed Sullivan Show" 20 times.

From the Twentieth Century Fox Television Series
ALLY McBEAL

SEARCHIN' MY SOUL

Words and Music by
VONDA SHEPARD

10

...end solo)

1.3. Whoa, I be - lieve I am read - y for what love____
2. Oh, I've been think - ing a - bout you for a long____

___ has___ to { bring._____ } I've got my - self to - geth -
___ time._   give._____
There's a sight in my

er. Now____ I'm read - y____ to { sing.__
life where__ I've been____ blind._ live.__

The Opening Title Theme from the HBO® series,
SEX AND THE CITY

SEX AND THE CITY
(Main Title Theme)

Music Composed by
DOUGLAS J. CUOMO

Bright latin ♩ = 157

Sex and the City - 2 - 1

From the HBO® Original Series "THE SOPRANOS"

WOKE UP THIS MORNING

Words and Music by
REV. D. WAYNE LOVE, CONGOMAN LOVE,
MOUNTAIN OF LOVE, LARRY LOVE
and CHESTER BURNETTE

one in a mil - lion, you've got to   burn to shine.___ But you were

born un-der a bad__ sign, with a   blue moon in your eyes."__ 2. Well, you   blue moon in your eyes.__ So, sing it now.

Chorus:

Woke up this   morn - ing.__   Got a   blue moon,   got a blue moon in your   eyes.____   So sad.

God - damn,__   a god-damn shame__ a-bout it.   Woke up this   morn - ing,__   got a

blue moon, got a blue moon in your eyes.___

1.

D.S. % 2.

You just can't help__ your - self.__

N.C.

Rap - see additional lyrics

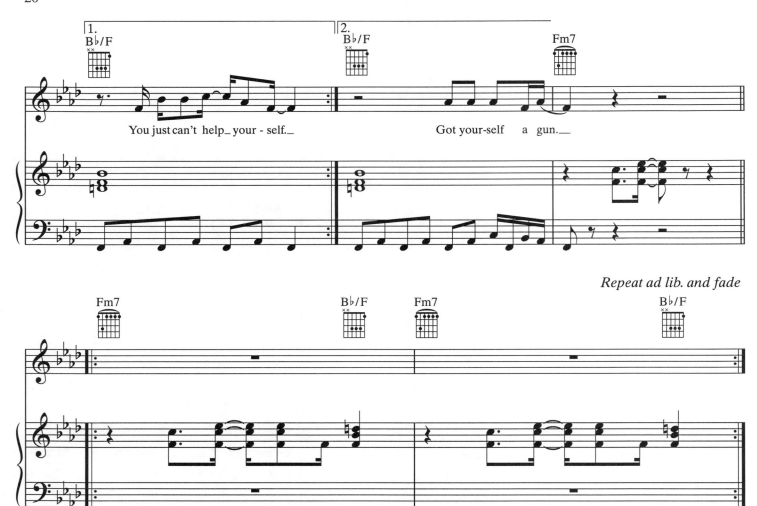

Repeat ad lib. and fade

Verse 2:
You woke up this morning,
All that love had gone.
Your papa never told you
About right and wrong.
But you're looking good, baby;
I believe you're feeling fine.
(Shame about it.)
Born under a bad sign
With a blue moon in your eyes.
So, sing it now.
(To Chorus:)

Verse 3:
You woke up this morning,
The world turned upside down.
Things ain't been the same
Since the blues walked into town.
But you're one in a million,
You've got that shotgun shine.
(Shame about it.)
Born under a bad sign
With a blue moon in your eyes.
(To Chorus:)

Rap:
When you woke up this morning, everything was gone.
By half past ten, your head was going ding-dong.
Ringing like a bell from your head down to your toes,
Like a voice telling you there's something you should know.
Last night you were flying, but today you're so low.
Ain't it times like these that make you wonder if you'll ever know
The meaning of things as they appear to others,
Wives, husbands, mothers, fathers, sisters, and brothers.
Don't you wish you didn't function?
Don't you wish you didn't think beyond the next paycheck
And the next little drink?
Well, you do, so make up your mind to go on.
'Cause when you woke up this morning,
Everything you had was gone.
(To Chorus:)

Theme from the TV Series "L.A. LAW"

L.A. LAW
(Main Title)

Music by MIKE POST

L.A. Law - 3 - 1

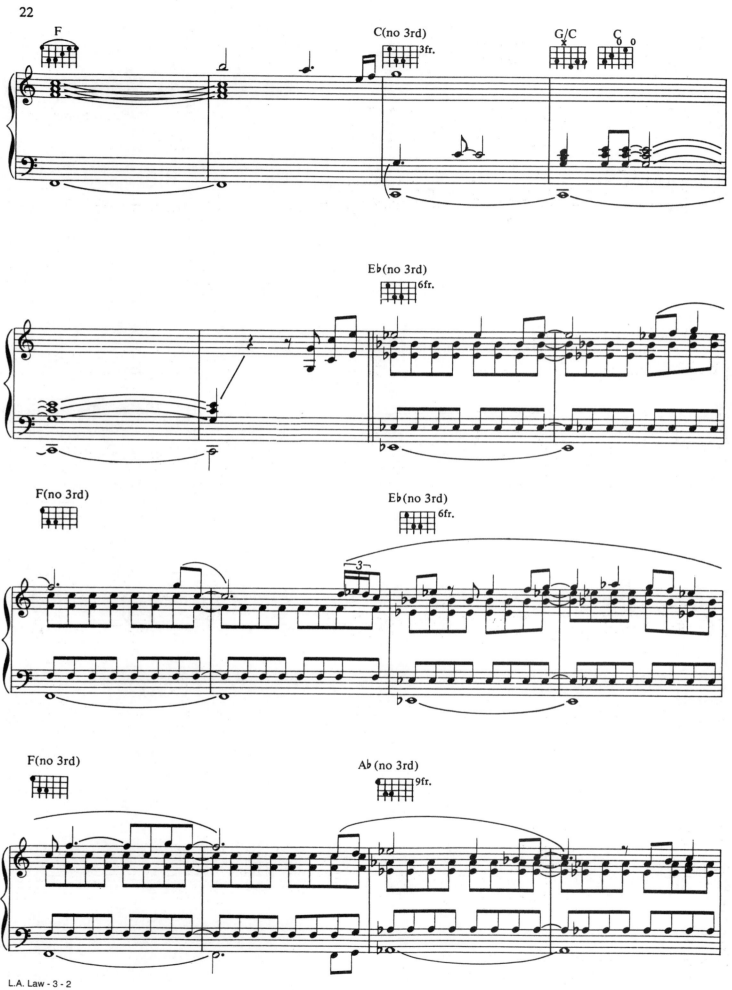

Theme from the Lorimar Productions, Inc. Televison Series "Dallas"

DALLAS

Music by
JERROLD IMMEL

Dallas - 4 - 1

Dallas - 4 - 2

Theme from the Lorimar Productions, Inc. TV Series "KNOT'S LANDING"

KNOT'S LANDING

Music by
JERROLD IMMEL

Knot's Landing - 2 - 1

29

Knot's Landing - 2 - 2

NORTHERN EXPOSURE

(Main Title)

Music by
DAVID SCHWARTZ

Northern Exposure - 2 - 1

Northern Exposure - 2 - 2

A 20th Century-Fox Series

THEME FROM "PEYTON PLACE"

Lyric by
PAUL FRANCIS WEBSTER

Music by
FRANZ WAXMAN

Theme From "Peyton Place" - 2 - 1

Theme From "Peyton Place" - 2 - 2

BAD BOYS
(Theme from "COPS")

Words and Music by
IAN LEWIS

Bad__ boys, what - 'cha want, what - 'cha want,

what - 'cha gon - na do__ when__ Sher-iff John Brown__ come for you?

Bad Boys - 5 - 1

Tell___ me what-'cha gon-na do, what-cha gon-na do - o. Bad

Chorus:

boys, bad boys, what-'cha gon-na do, What-'cha gon-na do when they come for you? Bad

boys, bad boys, what-'cha gon-na do, what-'cha gon-na do when they come for you? 1.When

36

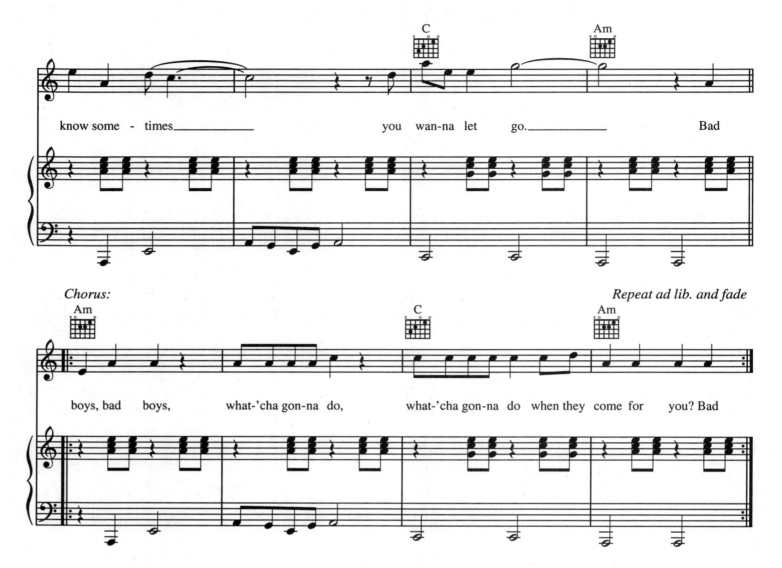

know some - times_____ you wan-na let go._____ Bad

Chorus:

Repeat ad lib. and fade

boys, bad boys, what-'cha gon-na do, what-'cha gon-na do when they come for you? Bad

Verse 2:
You chuck it on that one,
You chuck it on this one,
You chuck it on your mother
And you chuck it on your father.
You chuck it on your brother
And you chuck it on your sister,
You chuck it on that one
And you chuck it on me.
(To Chorus:)

Verse 3:
Nobody naw give you no breaks,
Police naw give you no breaks,
Soldier naw give you no breaks,
Not even your idren naw give you no breaks.
(To Chorus:)

Theme from the PBS Series "MASTERPIECE THEATRE"

THE MASTERPIECE

By
J.J. MOURET and
PAUL PARNES

The Masterpiece - 3 - 1

40

THE FUGITIVE

By
PETE RUGULO

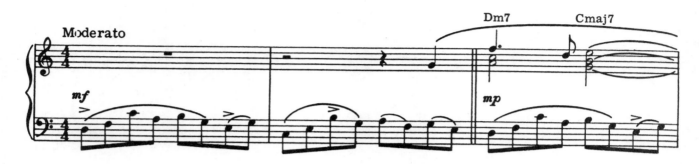

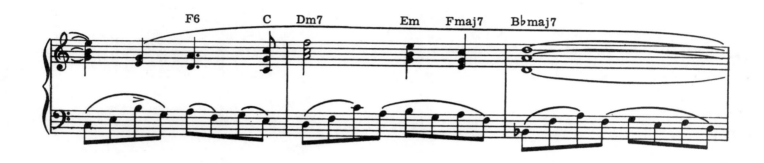

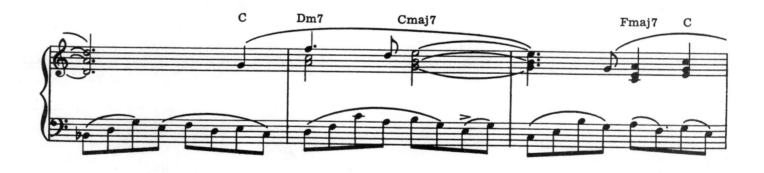

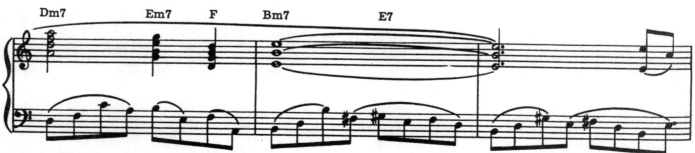

The Fugitive - 2 - 1

The Fugitive - 2 - 2

The Theme from
THE ANDY GRIFFITH SHOW

By
E. HAGEN and H. SPENCER

The Andy Griffith Show - 2 - 1

The Andy Griffith Show - 2 - 2

From the TV Series "FANTASY ISLAND"

THEME FROM FANTASY ISLAND

Music by
LAURENCE ROSENTHAL

Theme From Fantasy Island - 3 - 1

48

Theme From Fantasy Island - 3 - 3

THEME FROM "PICKET FENCES"

By
STEWART LEVIN

Theme From "Picket Fences" - 3 - 1

52

From the TV series "The West Wing"

THE WEST WING (MAIN TITLE)

Composed by
W.G. SNUFFY WALDEN

THEME FROM "MAGNUM, P.I."

from the Universal Television Series MAGNUM, P.I.

Music by
MIKE POST and PETE CARPENTER

Theme From "Magnum, P.I." - 5 - 1

54

Theme From "Magnum, P.I." - 5 - 3

Theme From "Magnum, P.I." - 5 - 5

MURDER, SHE WROTE

Theme from the Universal Television Series MURDER, SHE WROTE

Music by
JOHN ADDISON

Murder, She Wrote - 2 - 1

Murder, She Wrote - 2 - 2

SIMON AND SIMON
From the Television Series

Music by BARRY DeVORZON
and MICHAEL TOWERS

Simon and Simon - 2 - 1

CHARLIE'S ANGELS
(Main Title)

By
JACK ELLIOT and
ALLYN FERGUSON (BMI)

Charlie's Angels - 3 - 2

Theme from the Television Production "MR. LUCKY"

MR. LUCKY

Words by JAY LIVINGSTON and RAY EVANS
Music by HENRY MANCINI

66

He: They say I'm luck - y,
She: They say you're luck - y,

mis - ter luck - y guy and
mis - ter luck - y guy but

you're the dar - ling,
so - son am
rea - why. I.

They call us why. I.

rall. e dim

Theme from the TV Series "PETER GUNN"

PETER GUNN

By
HENRY MANCINI

Peter Gunn - 3 - 1

(R.H. ad lib. solo if desired)

loco

Peter Gunn - 3 - 3

THEME FROM "THE A-TEAM"

Words and Music by
MIKE POST and PETE CARPENTER

March ♩ = 120

Theme From "The A-Team" - 3 - 1

72

Theme From "The A-Team" - 3 - 2

Theme From "The A-Team" - 3 - 3

74

From the MTM Enterprises, Inc. Series "REMINGTON STEELE"

REMINGTON STEELE

Music by
HENRY MANCINI

Remington Steele - 2 - 1

THE ROCKFORD FILES

Music by MIKE POST
and PETE CARPENTER

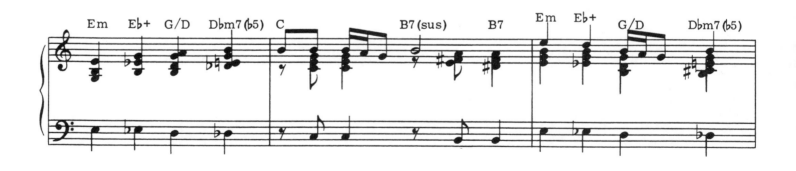

The Rockford Files - 2 - 1

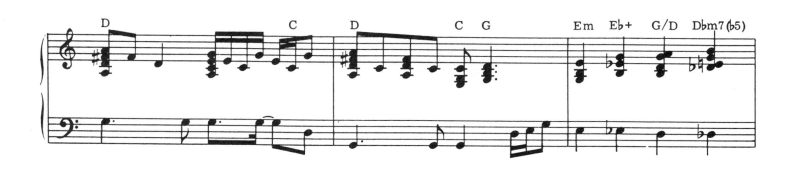

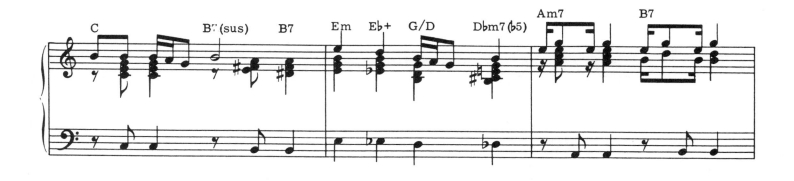

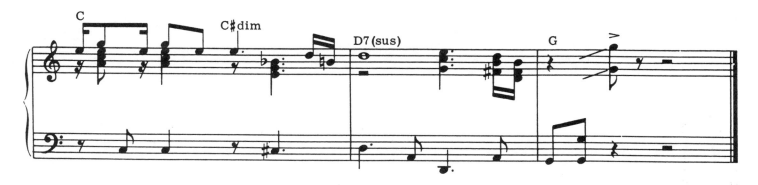

From the Television Show "AS THE WORLD TURNS"

IF THIS ISN'T LOVE

Words and Music by
GLORIA SKLEROV and STEVE DORFF

1. It must be fate that
2. Once in your life the

brought you to me that night.
right one will come a - long.

Two lone - ly hearts gone wrong.
In - side each oth - er's arms is the

sud - den - ly got it right.
place that we both be - long.

My de - fens - es came tum - bling down,
We knew it with - out a word,

I was
you

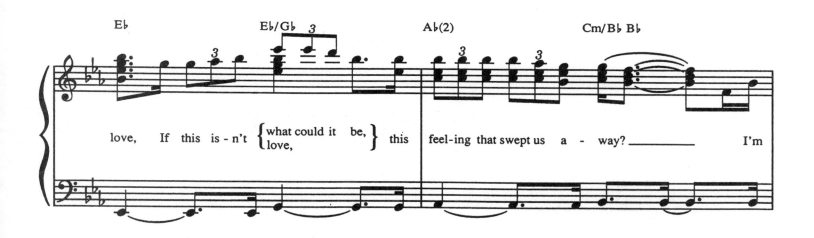

If This Isn't Love - 4 - 2

what it is, ___ ba - by. if this is - n't love. ___

D.S. 𝄋

what it is, ___ ba - by, if this is -

n't love. ___ *(Instrumental solo . . .*

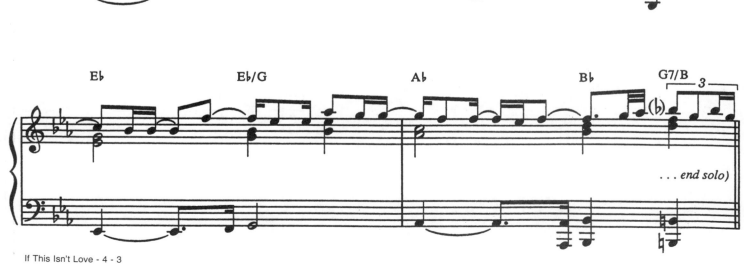

. . . end solo)

If This Isn't Love - 4 - 4

From the TV Series "NYPD BLUE"

THEME FROM "NYPD BLUE"

Music by
MIKE POST

Moderately fast

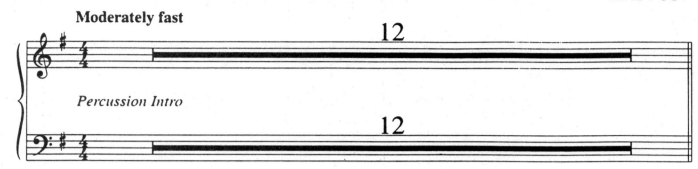

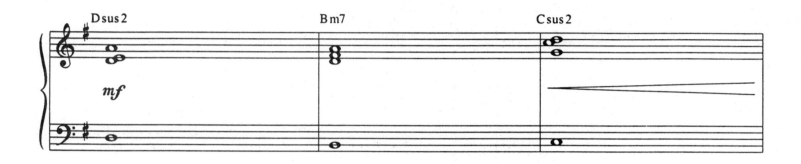

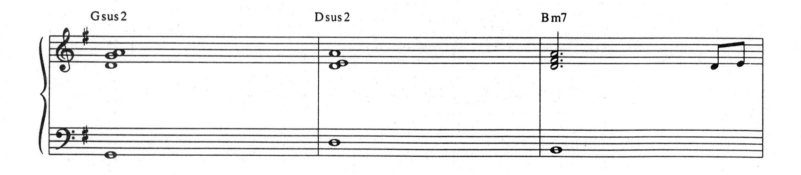

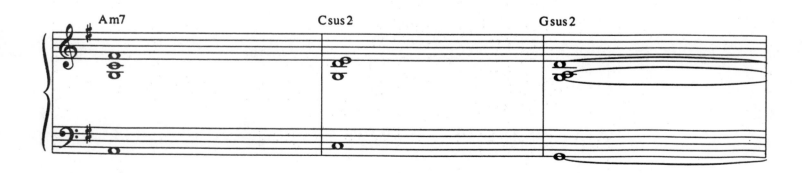

Theme From "NYPD Blue" - 2 - 1

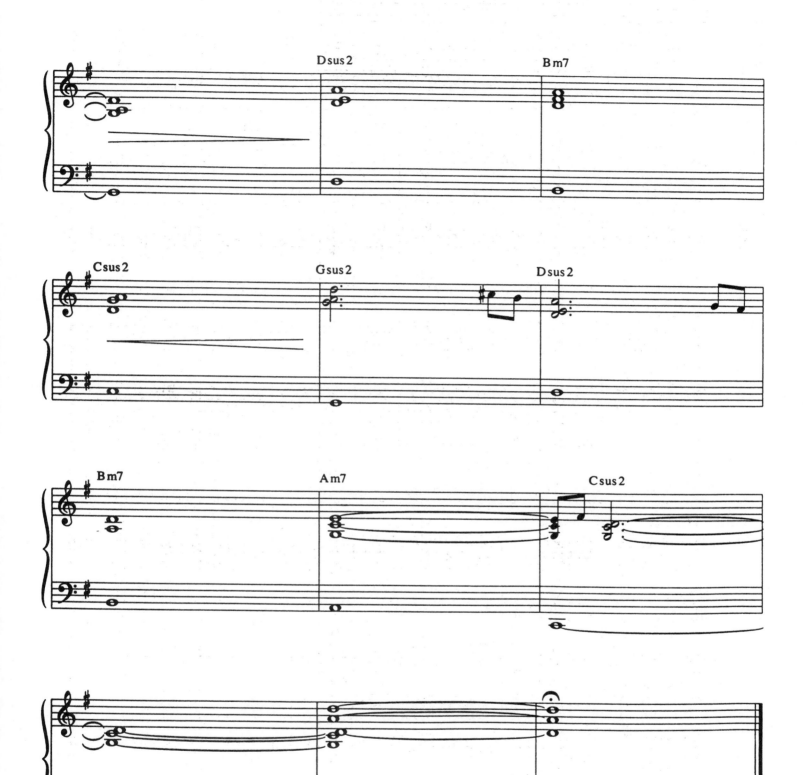

HAWAII FIVE-O

Music by
MORT STEVENS

Hawaii Five-O - 2 - 1

THE HILL STREET BLUES THEME

Music by
MIKE POST

The Hill Street Blues Theme - 2 - 1

The Hill Street Blues Theme - 2 - 2

Theme From the Universal Television Series

MIAMI VICE

By JAN HAMMER

Miami Vice - 4 - 1

T. J. HOOKER
(Main Title)

Music by
MARK SNOW

Brightly ♩ = 144

T. J. Hooker - 2 - 1

Television Theme From

THE MOD SQUAD

Music by
EARLE HAGEN

Moderato - with a beat

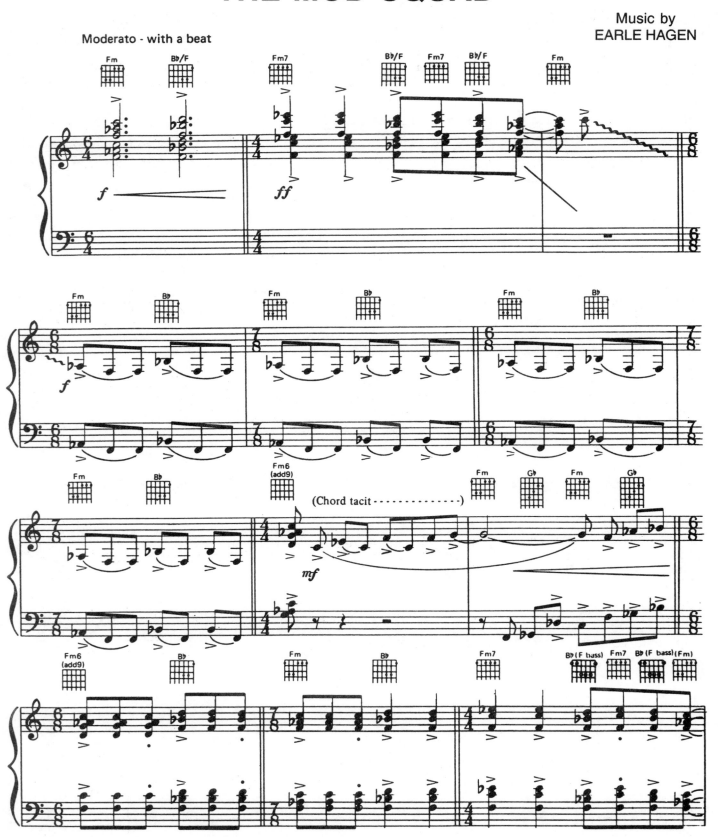

The Mod Squad - 4 - 1

96

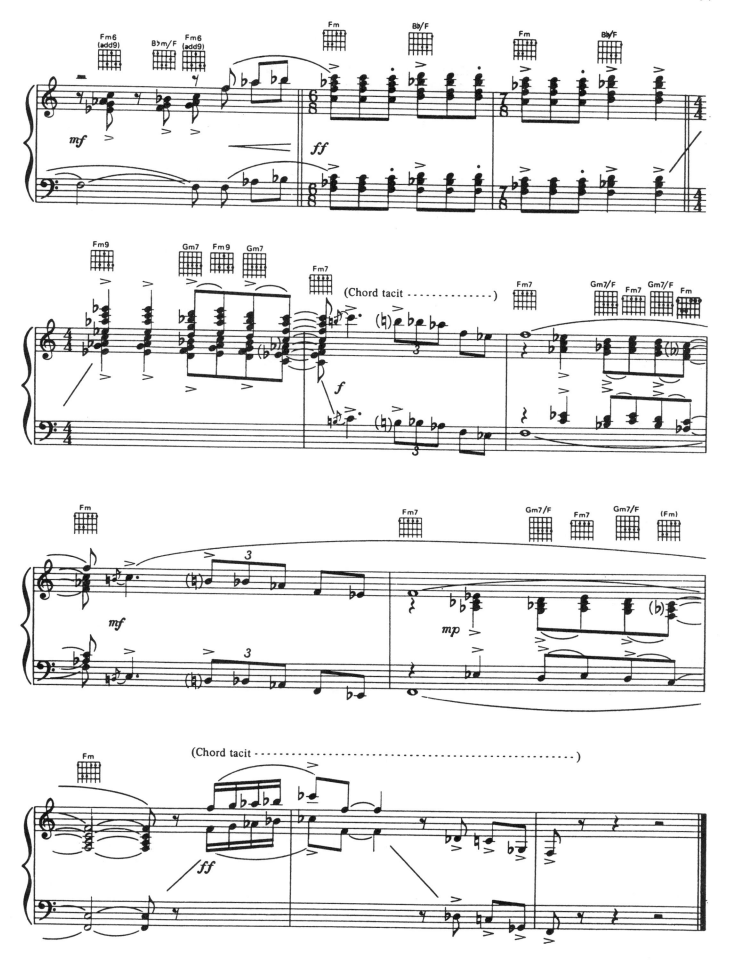

THEME FROM "HUNTER"

Music by
MIKE POST and PETE CARPENTER

From the TV Show "JEOPARDY"
JEOPARDY THEME

Music by
MERV GRIFFIN

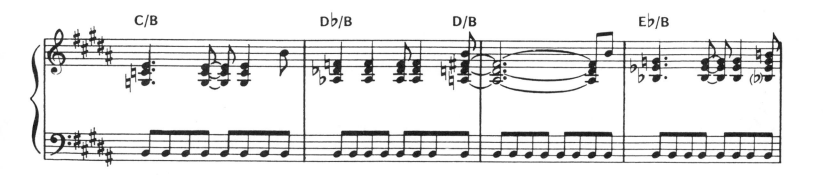

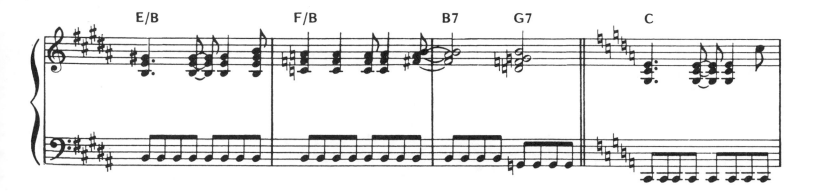

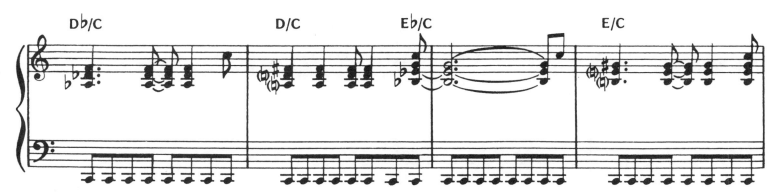

Jeopardy Theme - 3 - 1

102

Jeopardy Theme - 3 - 2

Jeopardy Theme - 3 - 3

Theme From "WHEEL OF FORTUNE"

CHANGING KEYS

Music by
MERV GRIFFIN

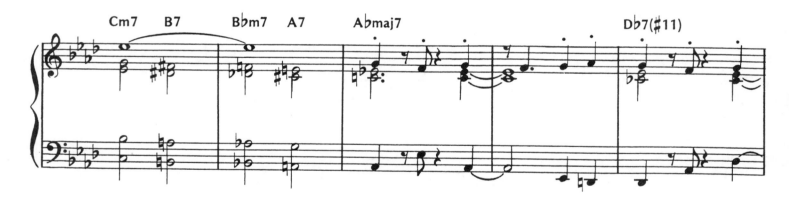

Changing Keys - 4 - 1

106

LAW AND ORDER

Music by
MIKE POST

Law and Order - 2 - 1

PERRY MASON THEME
From the Television Series

Music by FRED STEINER

(senza 8va)

(con 8va – ad lib.)

(senza 8va)

1.

D.S. 𝄋

2.

sfp

rallent.

THEME FROM "MURDER ONE"

Music by
MIKE POST

Theme From "Murder One" - 2 - 2

WALK WITH YOU
(Theme from "Touched By An Angel")

Music and Lyrics by
MARC LICHTMAN

D D♯dim Em C Dsus G
Walk with you, 'til the sun don't shine.
D D♯dim Em C C/D D D♯dim Em
Walk with you, ev - 'ry time. Walk with you, 'til the
C G D D♯dim Em C/D
clouds fade a - way. Walk with you, each and ev - 'ry day, I will
G C G
walk with you. Be-lieve me, I'll walk with you.

Theme From

DR. QUINN, MEDICINE WOMAN

By
WILLIAM OLVIS

From the MGM-TV & NBC-TV Production "DR. KILDAIRE"

THEME FROM "DR. KILDAIRE"

(Three Stars Will Shine Tonight)

Lyric by
HAL WYNN

Music by
JERRALD GOLDSMITH
and PETE RUGOLO

Lyrics:
Three Stars Will Shine To-night, one for the lone-ly,

That star will shine its light each time that some - one sighs.

Three stars for all to see, one for young lov - ers,

Theme From "Dr. Kildaire" - 2 - 1

Theme From "Dr. Kildaire" - 2 - 2

ER
(Main Theme)

Composed by
JAMES NEWTON HOWARD

ER - 2 - 1

Theme From the TV Series "CHICAGO HOPE"

THEME FROM "CHICAGO HOPE"

Music by
MARK ISHAM

Theme From "Chicago Hope" - 2 - 1

From the "TONY ORLANDO & DAWN SHOW"

TIE A YELLOW RIBBON
'ROUND THE OLE OAK TREE

Words and Music by
IRWIN LEVINE and L. RUSSELL BROWN

Tie a Yellow Ribbon 'Round the Ole Oak Tree - 4 - 1

Tie a Yellow Ribbon 'Round the Ole Oak Tree - 4 - 2

128

Tie a Yellow Ribbon 'Round the Ole Oak Tree - 4 - 4

THE SYNCOPATED CLOCK

Words by
MITCHELL PARISH

Music by
LEROY ANDERSON

The Syncopated Clock - 4 - 1

132

ex-perts came to hear and see, But none of them could solve the mys-ter-y, They

called Pro-fes-sor Ein-stein too, He said "There's noth-ing I can do." But soon the fick-le

hu-man race will find an-oth-er freak to take its place, And one fine day the

man will hock the poor old SYN-CO-PAT-ED CLOCK.

From the Twentieth Century Fox Television Series

KING OF THE HILL

Words and Music by
ROGER CLYNE, BRIAN BLUSH,
ARTHUR EDWARDS and PAUL NAFFAH

King of the Hill - 2 - 1

From the Twentieth Century Fox Television Series FAMILY GUY

THEME FROM FAMILY GUY

Music and Lyrics by
WALTER MURPHY

Theme From Family Guy - 2 - 1

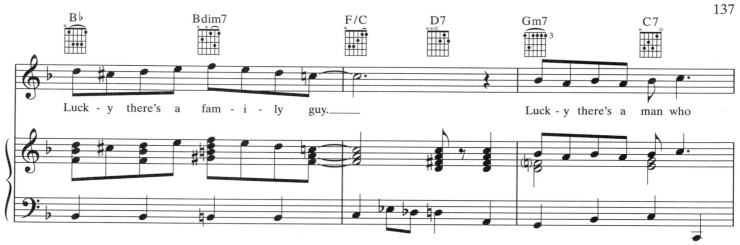

Luck - y there's a fam - i - ly guy._____ Luck - y there's a man who

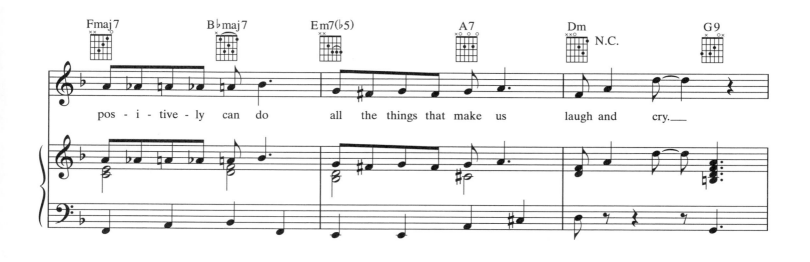

pos - i - tive - ly can do all the things that make us laugh and cry.___

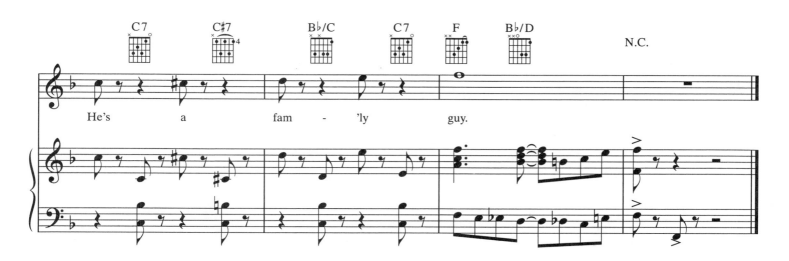

He's a fam - 'ly guy.

THEME FROM "THE SIMPSONS"

Music by
DANNY ELFMAN

Theme From "The Simpsons" - 4 - 1

Theme From "The Simpsons" - 4 - 2

140

a tempo

Theme From "The Simpsons" - 4 - 4

From the Twentieth Century Fox Television Series FUTURAMA

THEME FROM FUTURAMA

Composed by
CHRISTOPHER TYNG

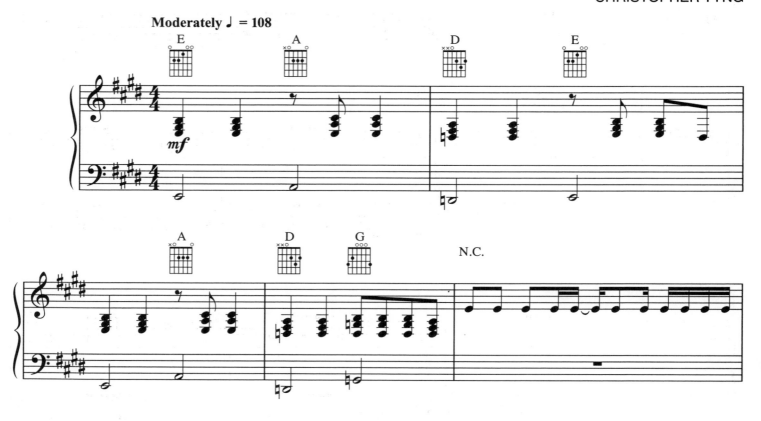

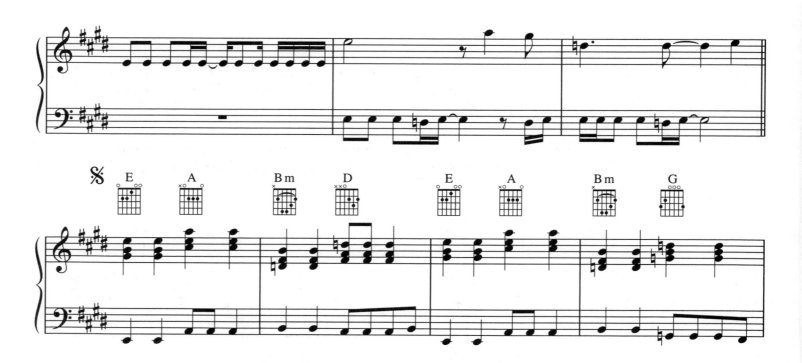

Theme From Futurama - 3 - 1

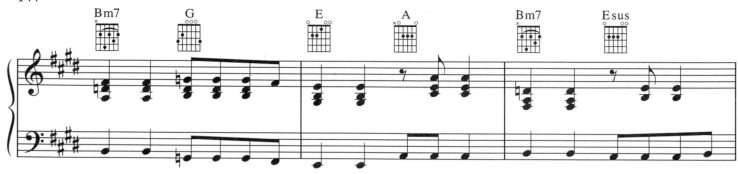

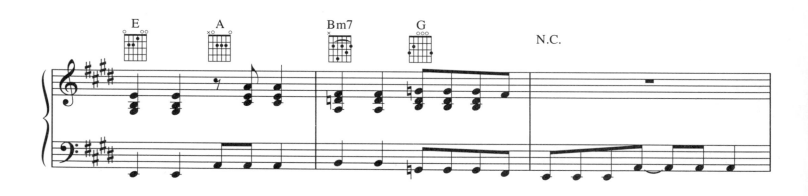

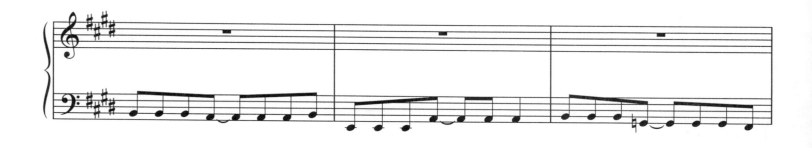

A Greenway Production in Association with 20th Century-Fox TV for ABC-TV

BATMAN THEME

Words and Music by
NEAL HEFTI

Batman Theme - 3 - 1

146

Batman Theme - 3 - 2

THE MUNSTERS THEME

From the Television Series

Music by
JACK MARSHALL

Moderately Slow

The Munsters Theme - 2 - 1

149

The Munsters Theme - 2 - 2

Theme From
THE X-FILES

Music by
MARK SNOW

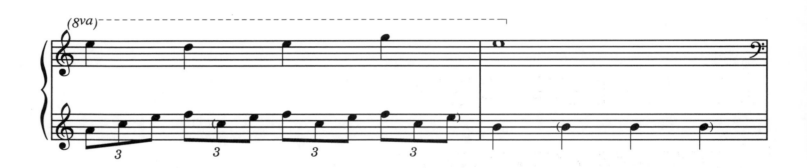

Theme From The X-Files - 6 - 1

151

Theme From The X-Files - 6 - 2

152

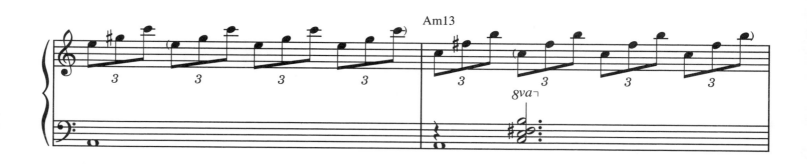

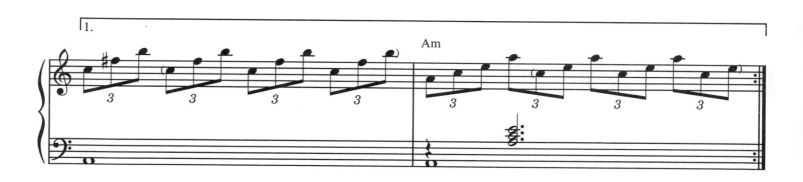

Theme From The X-Files - 6 - 3

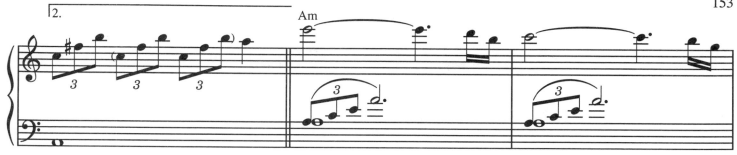

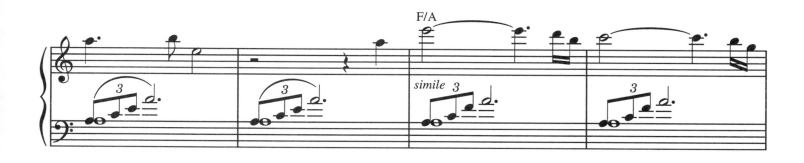

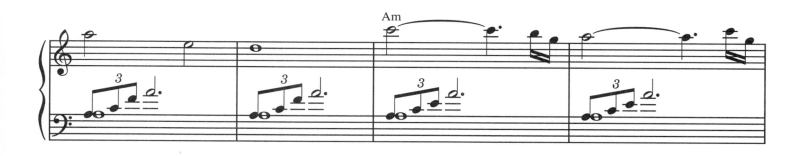

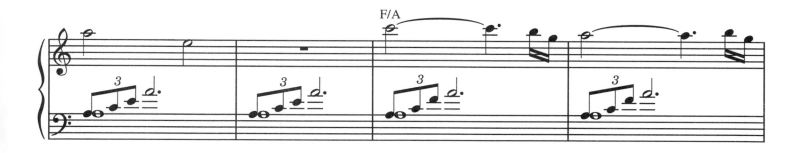

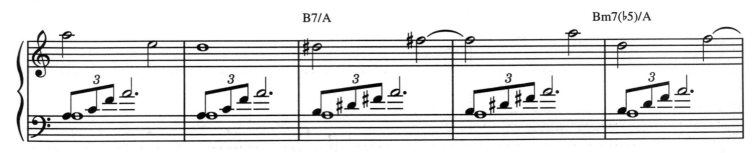

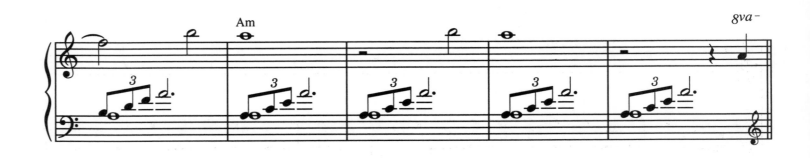

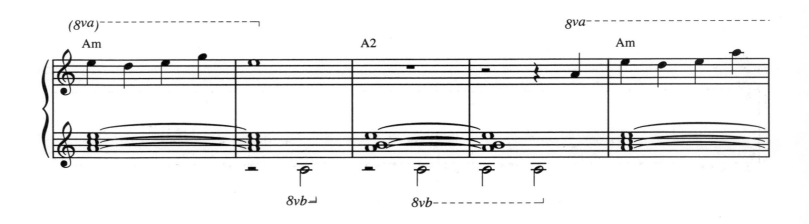

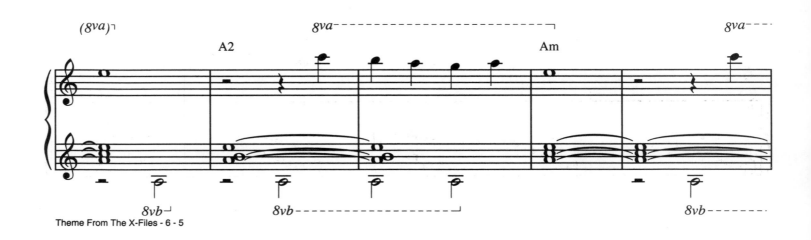

Theme From The X-Files - 6 - 5

From the Twentieth Century Fox Television Series

MILLENNIUM

Composed by
MARK SNOW

Moderately ♩ = 120

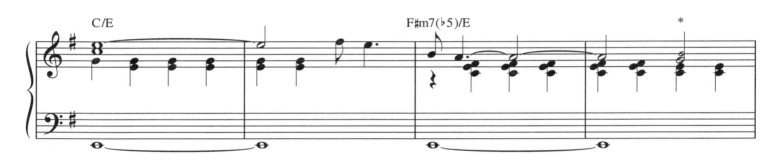

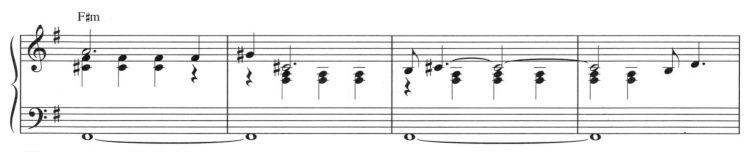

*Play cue note melody 2nd time.

158

simile

Millennium - 4 - 3

QUANTUM LEAP

Music by
MIKE POST

Moderately bright rock ♩ = 144

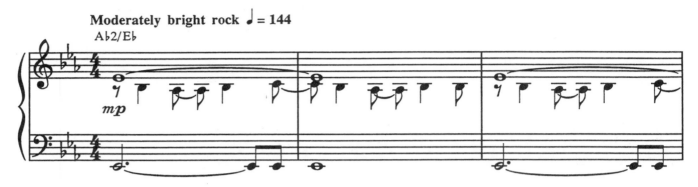

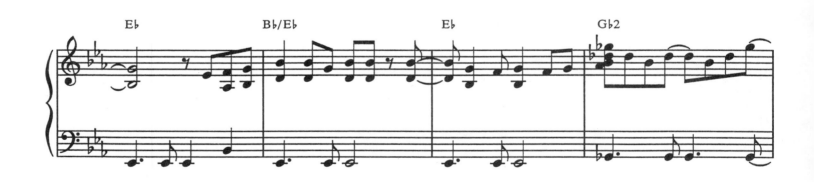

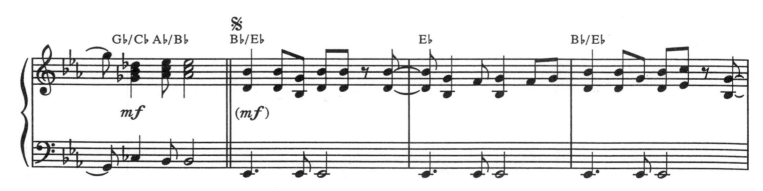

Quantum Leap - 2 - 1

TWILIGHT ZONE

Music by
MARIUS CONSTANT

Twilight Zone - 2 - 1

*Notes or directions in parentheses are things that were in the original TV arrangement, but must be omitted in order that the arrangement be playable on the piano.

Twilight Zone - 2 - 2

THE POWERPUFF GIRLS
(END THEME)

Words and Music by
AMANDA McKINNON, STEVEN CLARK,
JOHN CLARK, THOMAS CHASE,
STEVEN RUCKER and JAMES L. VENABLE

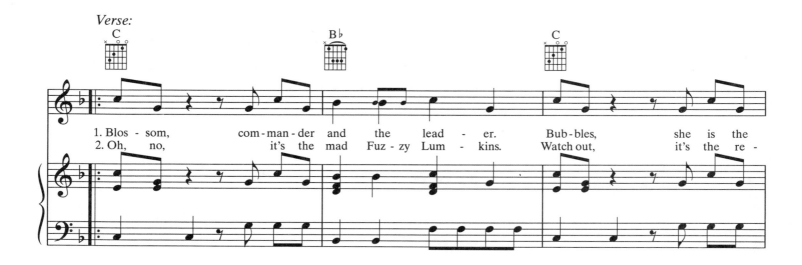

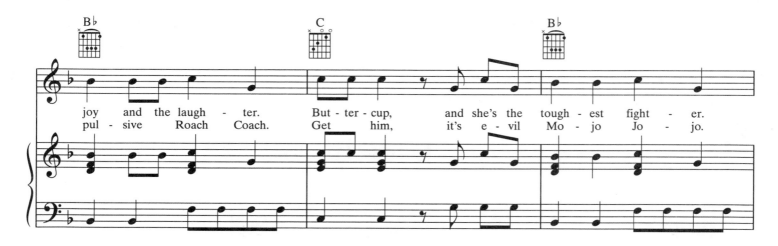

The Powerpuff Girls (End Theme) - 3 - 1

The Powerpuff Girls (End Theme) - 3 - 2

Theme from "THE BUGS BUNNY SHOW"

THIS IS IT!

Words and Music by
MACK DAVID and JERRY LIVINGSTON

This Is It! - 3 - 1

WOODY WOODPECKER

From the Cartoon Television Series

Words and Music by
GEORGE TIBBLES and RAMEY IDRISS

Woody Woodpecker - 4 - 2

I TAUT I TAW A PUDDY-TAT
(I Thought I Saw a Pussy-Cat)

Words and Music by
ALAN LIVINGSTON, BILLY MAY and WARREN FOSTER

I Taut I Taw a Puddy-Tat - 2 - 1

Additional Lyrics

2. There is a great big bad old cat,
Sylvester is his name,
He only has one aim in life,
And that is very plain.
He dreams of catching Tweety Pie
And eating him one day,
But just as he gets close enough.
Tweety gets away:
                                    Chorus:

3. Tweety sometimes takes a walk
And goes outside his cage,
But he gets back before the cat,
And throws him in a rage.
Sylvester'd love to eat that bird
If he could just get near,
But ev'rytime that he comes by,
This is all he'll hear:
                                    Chorus:

4. And when he sings that little song,
His mistress knows he's home,
She grabs her broom and brings it down
Upon Sylvester's dome.
So there's no need of worrying,
He lives just like a king,
And puddy tats can't hurt that bird
As long at he can sing:
                                    Chorus:

WAKKO'S AMERICA

Lyrics by
RANDY ROGEL

TRADITIONAL

178

180

(MEET) THE FLINTSTONES
from THE FLINTSTONES

Words and Music by
WILLIAM HANNA, JOSEPH BARBERA
and HOYT CURTIN

Theme from the Warner Bros. Animated TV Series "FREE WILLY"

FREE WILLY

Words and Music by
MICHAEL KAMEN

Free Willy - 3 - 1

188

Free Willy - 3 - 3

JETSONS MAIN THEME
from THE JETSONS

Words and Music by WILLIAM HANNA,
JOSEPH BARBERA and HOYT CURTIN

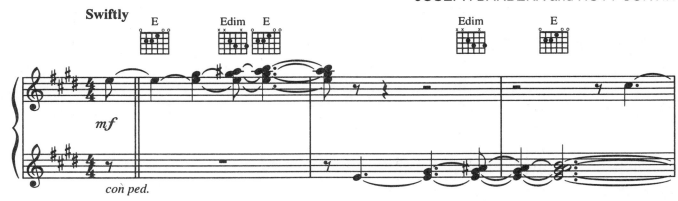

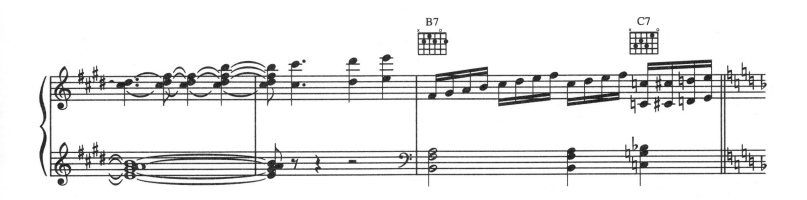

Meet George Jet - son!

Jetsons Main Theme - 3 - 1

190

(Spoken:) And

Ro - sy, the ro - bot maid. ___

HUCKLEBERRY HOUND
from the Cartoon Television Series

Words and Music by WILLIAM HANNA,
JOSEPH BARBERA and HOYT CURTIN

Fast march

The big-gest show in town is Huck-le-ber-ry Hound for all you guys and gals. The big-gest clown in town is Huck-le-ber-ry Hound with all his car-toon pals. It's Huck-le-

Huckleberry Hound - 2 - 1

Theme Song from the Mirisch-G&E Production, "THE PINK PANTHER," a United Artists Release

THE PINK PANTHER

Music by
HENRY MANCINI

Moderately Mysterioso

The Pink Panther - 2 - 1

SCOOBY DOO MAIN TITLE
from the Cartoon Television Series

Words and Music by
WILLIAM HANNA, JOSEPH BARBERA
and HOYT CURTAIN

Up-tempo

1. Scoo-by Doo-by Doo, look-in' for you. Scoo-by Doo-by Doo, where are ya?
2. (Instrumental solo...

...solo ends)

All ___ the stars are here wait-
Na ___ na na na na na ___

Scooby Doo Main Title - 2 - 1

THEME FROM "THE ROAD RUNNER"

By
BARBARA CAMERON

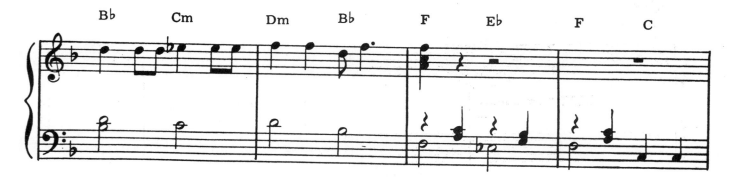

Theme From "The Road Runner" - 2 - 1

199

Theme From "The Road Runner" - 2 - 2

TINY TOON ADVENTURES
Theme Song

Lyrics by
WAYNE KAATZ, TOM RUEGGER
and BRUCE BROUGHTON

Music by
BRUCE BROUGHTON

YOGI BEAR SONG

From the Cartoon Television Series

Words and Music by WILLIAM HANNA
JOSEPH BARBERA and HOYT S. CURTIN

Yo - gi Bear is smart-er than the av - 'rage bear. Yo - gi Bear is al - ways in the rang - er's hair. At a pic - nic ta - ble, you will find him there, stuff - in' down more good-ies than the

MERRILY WE ROLL ALONG

Words and Music by
EDDIE CANTOR, MURRAY MENCHER
and CHARLIE TOBIAS

Merrily We Roll Along - 2 - 1

205

THE MERRY-GO-ROUND BROKE DOWN

Words and Music by
CLIFF FRIEND and DAVE FRANKLIN

The Merry-Go-Round Broke Down - 2 - 2

JOSIE AND THE PUSSYCATS
MAIN TITLE
(from the Cartoon Television Series)

Words and Music by
HOYT CURTIN, DENBY WILLIAMS
and JOSEPH ROLAND

Jo - sie and the Pus-sy - cats, long tails and ears for hats, gui - tars and sharps 'n' flats. Neat, sweet, a groov-y song, you're in - vit - ed, come a - long.

Josie and the Pussycats - 3 - 1

Main Title from "MIGHTY MORPHIN POWER RANGERS"

GO GO POWER RANGERS

(Mighty Morphin Power Rangers Main Title)

Words and Music by
SHUKI LEVY and KUSSA MAHCHI

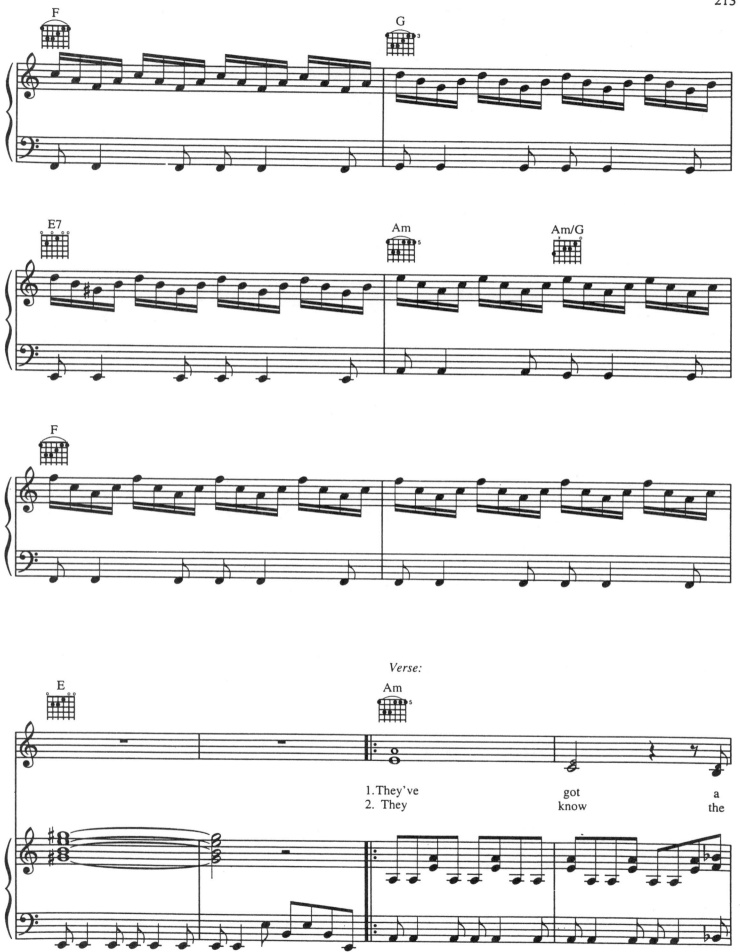

214

Go Go Power Rangers - 9 - 5

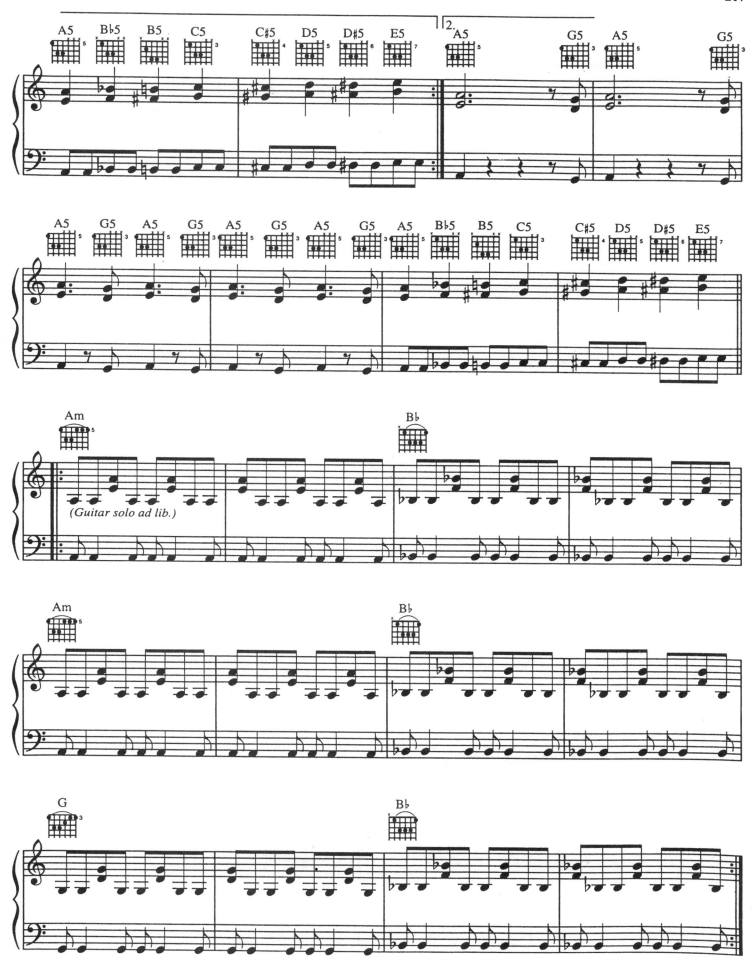

218

Based on a Theme from the Warner Bros. TV Movie "THE THORN BIRDS"

ANYWHERE THE HEART GOES

(Meggie's Theme)

Words by
WILL JENNINGS

Music by
HENRY MANCINI

You know I will fol - low an - y - where the heart goes. I will go un - til I've known all life can be. _____

Anywhere the Heart Goes - 3 - 1

THEME FROM "GENERAL HOSPITAL"

Words and Music by
JACK URBONT

Moderately fast ♩ = 138

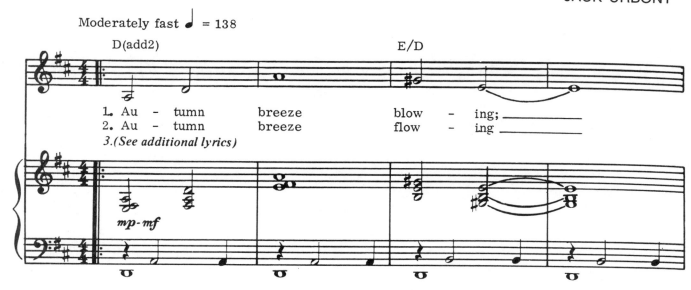

1. Au - tumn breeze blow - ing; _____
2. Au - tumn breeze flow - ing _____
3. (See additional lyrics)

wind of whis - p'ring sighs. _____ I can't help
like a mel - o - dy. _____ I can't help

know - ing _____ you're blow - ing me a _ sur - prise. _____
glow - ing, _____ know - ing _ what you bring _ to

224

Verse 3:
Gentle breeze, guide me
Through life's stormy seas
Till my love's beside me,
Softly, I'll pray on my knees.
Blow me my one true love,
Autumn breeze.

SECRET AGENT MAN

Words and Music by
P.F. SLOAN and STEVE BARRI

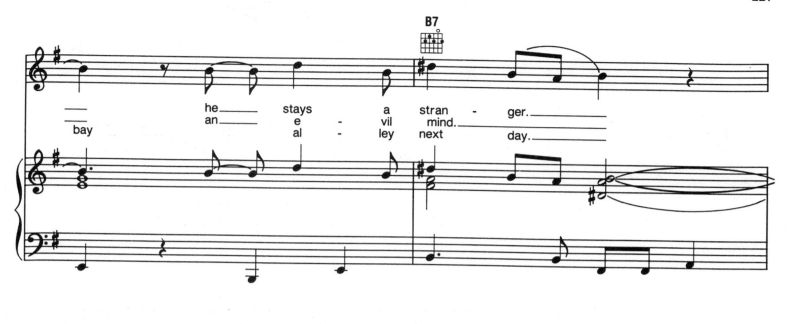

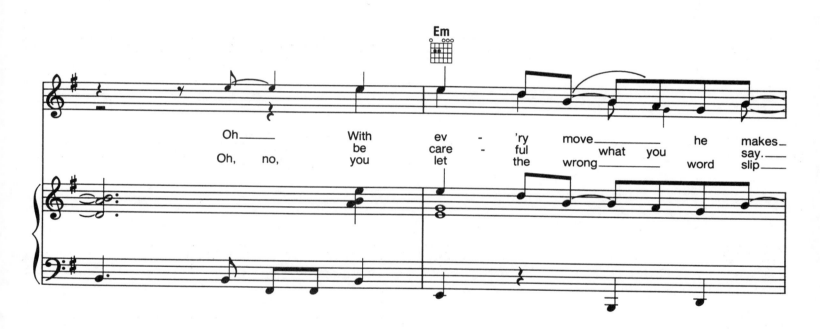

Secret Agent Man - 4 - 2

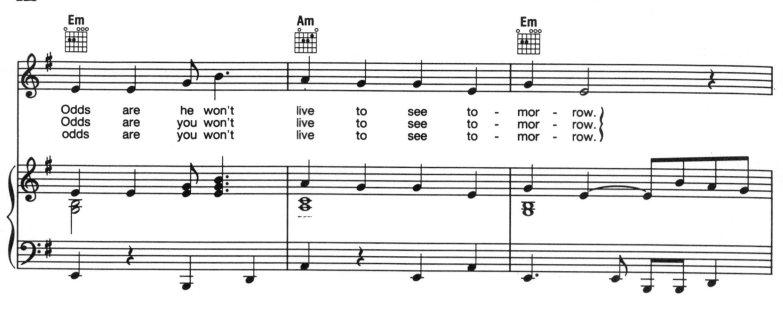

Odds are he won't live to see to - mor - row.
Odds are you won't live to see to - mor - row.
odds are you won't live to see to - mor - row.

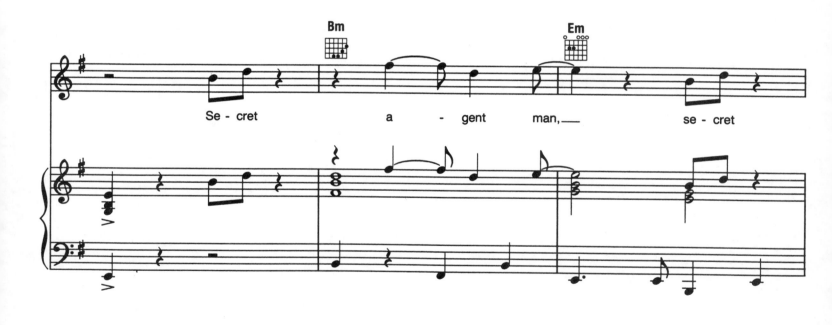

Se - cret a - gent man,___ se - cret

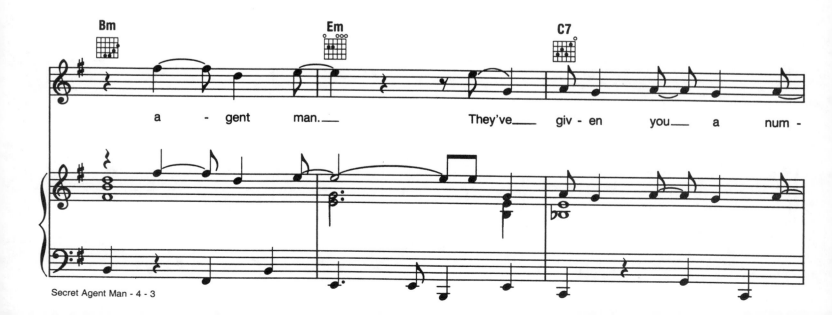

a - gent man.___ They've___ giv - en you___ a num -

Secret Agent Man - 4 - 3

From the VH1 Original Movie AT ANY COST

PINCH ME

Words and Music by
STEVEN PAGE and ED ROBERTSON

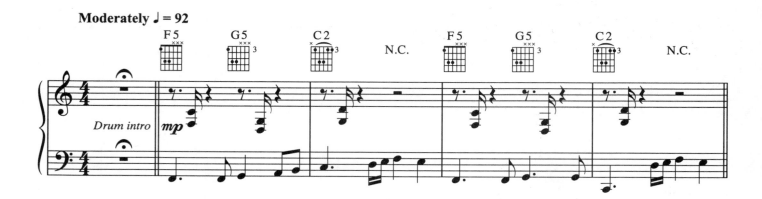

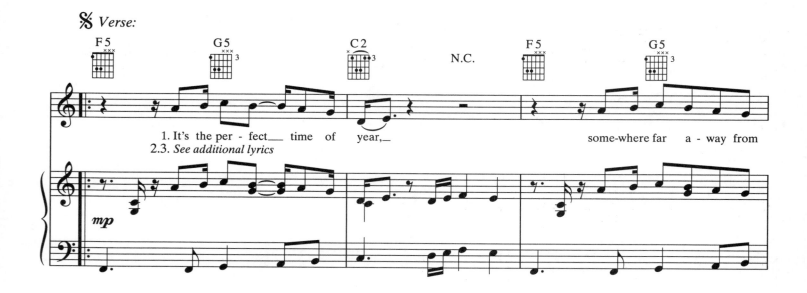

Pinch Me - 7 - 1

232

Chorus:

It's like a dream, you try to re-mem-ber, but it's gone, then you try to scream, but it on-ly comes out as a yawn, when you

tacet 1x

Pinch me. Pinch me,

try to see the world be-yond your front door.

I'm still a - sleep.

To Coda

Take your time 'cause the way I rhyme's gon-na make you smile, when you re-al-ize that a guy my size might take a while, just to

Please, God, tell me

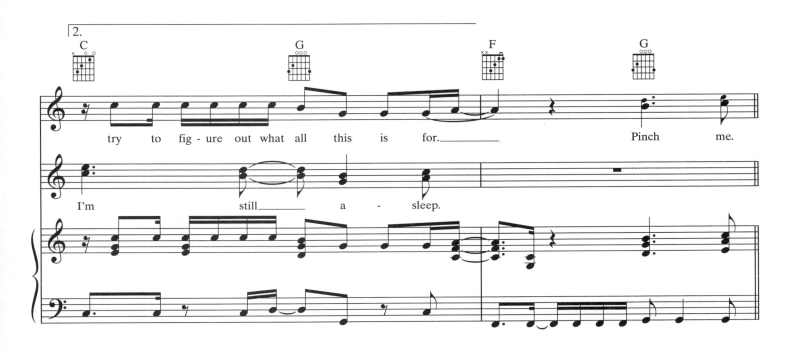

Bridge:

234

Pinch Me - 7 - 5

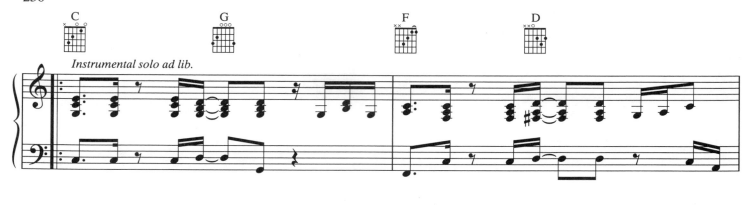

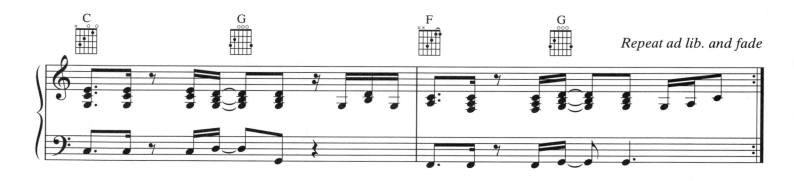

Repeat ad lib. and fade

Verse 2:
It's the perfect time of day
To throw all your cares away;
Put the sprinkler on the lawn
And run through with my gym shorts on.
Take a drink right from the hose
And change into some dryer clothes;
Climb the stairs up to my room,
Sleep away the afternoon.
(To Chorus:)

Verse 3:
On an evening such as this,
It's hard to tell if I exist.
If I pack the car and leave this town,
Who'll notice that I'm not around?
I could hide out under there.
(I just made you say underwear.)
I could leave but I'll just stay,
All my stuff's here anyway.
(To Chorus:)

LATE SHOW THEME

By
PAUL SHAFFER

238

Late Show Theme - 3 - 2

From the NBC Production "LATE NIGHT WITH DAVID LETTERMAN"

VIEWER MAIL THEME

Music by
HENRY MANCINI

Viewer Mail Theme - 2 - 1

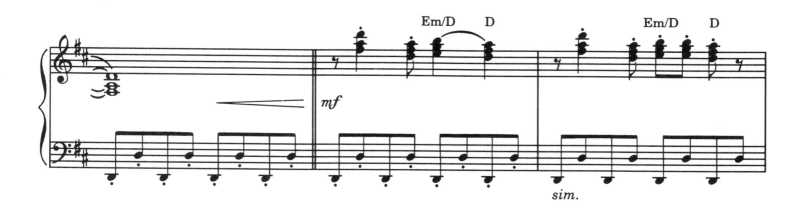

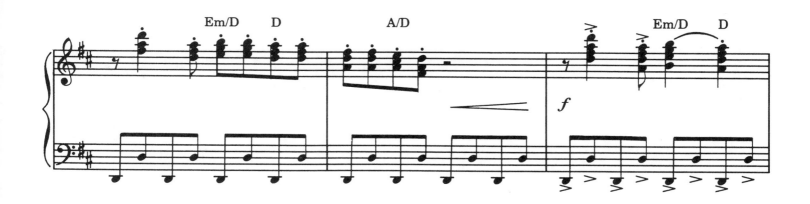

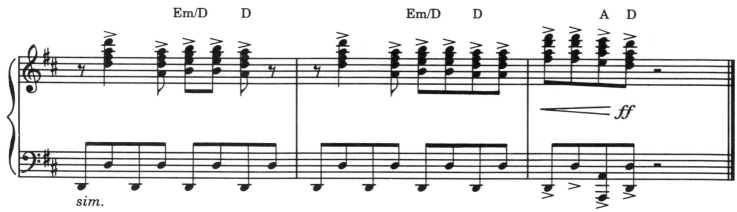

Viewer Mail Theme - 2 - 2

(Theme from)
THE ROSIE O'DONNELL SHOW

Music by
JOHN McDANIEL
Words by
RANDY COHEN

The Rosie O'Donnell Show - 3 - 1

244

From the 20th Century Fox Television Series

DHARMA & GREG
(Main Title)

Composed by
DENNIS C. BROWN

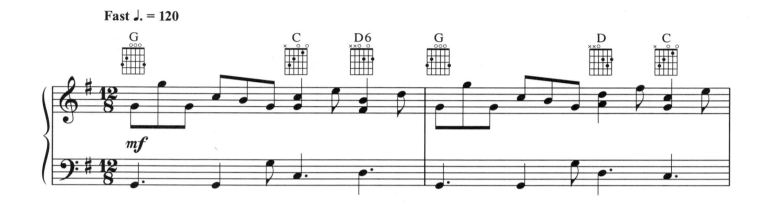

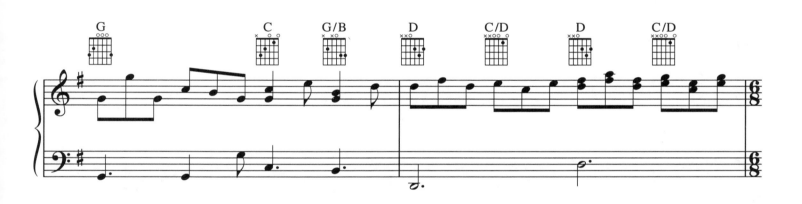

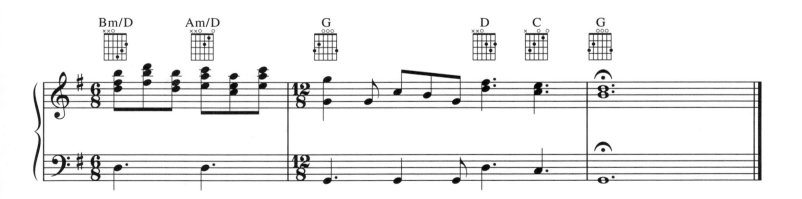

EVERYBODY LOVES RAYMOND
(Main Title)

By
RICK MAROTTA
and TERRY TROTTER

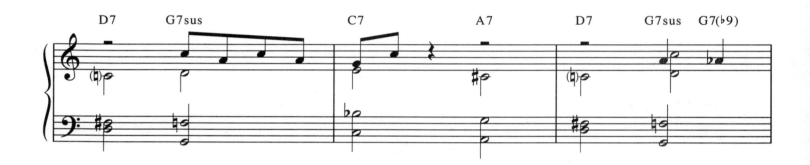

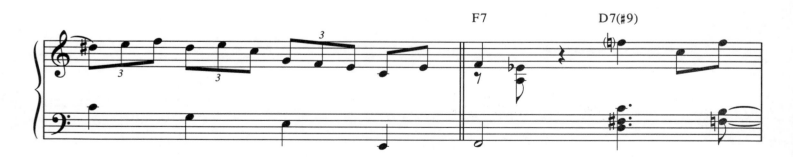

Everybody Loves Raymond - 2 - 1

Theme From "GROWING PAINS"

AS LONG AS WE GOT EACH OTHER

Words by
JOHN BETTIS

Music by
STEVE DORFF

Show me that smile a-gain, don't waste an-oth-er min-
When-ev-er skies are grey I look in-to your eyes

Instrumental

ute on your cry-in'. We're no-where near the end, the best
and see them shin-in'. Hold-ing you close this way is like

As Long As We Got Each Other - 4 - 1

Theme From "GILLIGAN'S ISLAND" TV Series

THE BALLAD OF GILLIGAN'S ISLE

Words and Music by
SHERWOOD SCHWARTZ and GEORGE WYLE

The Ballad of Gilligan's Isle - 2 - 1

BOSS OF ME
(Theme from "Malcolm in the Middle")

Words and Music by
JOHN FLANSBURGH
and JOHN LINNELL

Boss of Me - 6 - 1

Boss of Me - 6 - 4

258

You're not the boss of me__ now, and you're not so big.

From the Dick Van Dyke TV Show

DICK VAN DYKE THEME

By
EARLE HAGEN

Dick Van Dyke Theme - 2 - 1

Dick Van Dyke Theme - 2 - 2

From the Steven Bochco Productions TV Series "DOOGIE HOWSER, M.D."

DOOGIE HOWSER, M.D.

Music by
MIKE POST

Doogie Howser, M.D. - 2 - 1

FACTS OF LIFE

Moderately, with a shuffle feel

Words and Music by
ALAN THICKE, GLORIA LORING
and AL BURTON

1. You take the good you take the bad; you take 'em both and there you have the facts of life, the facts of life. There's a time you got-ta go and show you're grow-in'. Now you know a-bout the facts of life, the facts

some-one that you care a-bout, it real-ly is-n't fair; they're out to slow you up, when you're grow-in' up. When you let 'em flirt and then you hurt, or wait-in' 'cause your date is late show-in' up, and you're

Facts of Life - 5 - 1

Theme From the TV Series "Married...With Children"

LOVE AND MARRIAGE

Lyric by
SAMMY CAHN

Music by
JAMES VAN HEUSEN

Schottische tempo

mf

LOVE AND MAR - RIAGE,   LOVE   AND   MAR - RIAGE,

Go to-geth - er like   a   horse and car - riage, This I tell ya
It's an in - sti - tute you   can't dis - par - age, ask the lo - cal

Love and Marriage - 3 - 1

LOVE AND MAR-RIAGE, LOVE AND MAR-RIAGE, Go to-geth-er like a horse and car-riage, Dad was told by moth - er, You can't have one, You can't have none, You can't have one with-out the oth - er!

Theme From TriStar Television's "MAD ABOUT YOU"

FINAL FRONTIER

Words and Music by
PAUL REISER and DON WAS

Final Frontier - 2 - 1

Theme From the TV Series "GOMER PYLE"

GOMER PYLE

Music by
EARLE HAGEN

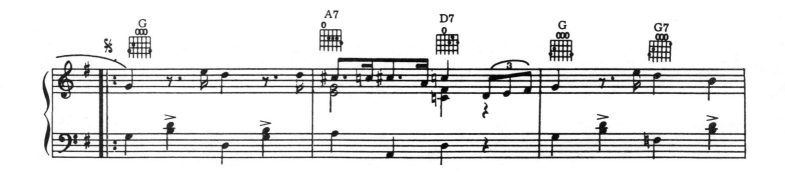

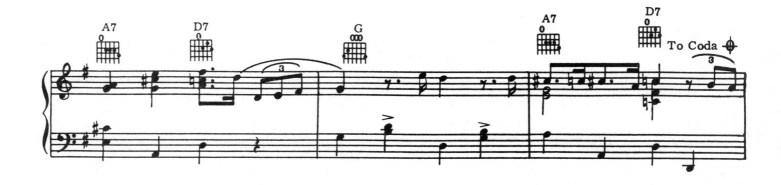

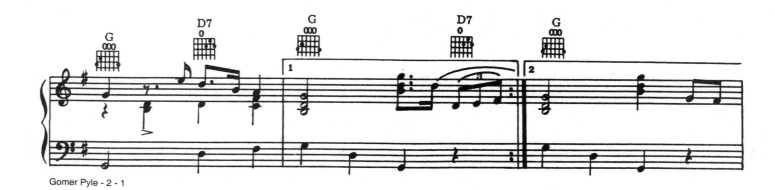

Gomer Pyle - 2 - 1

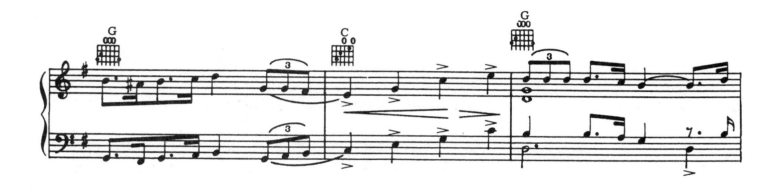

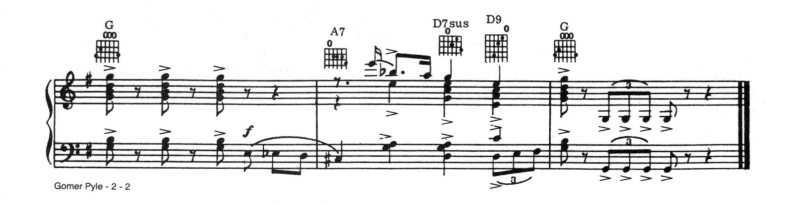

Gomer Pyle - 2 - 2

I'LL BE THERE FOR YOU

(Theme from "Friends")

Words by
DAVID CRANE, MARTA KAUFFMAN,
ALLEE WILLIS, PHIL SOLEM
and DANNY WILDE

Music by
MICHAEL SKLOFF

I'll Be There for You - 6 - 1

* Guitar fill reads 8va.

I'll Be There for You - 6 - 3

er know— me, no one could ev - er see— me.

Seems you're the on - ly one— who knows— what it's

like to be— me. Some - one to face— the day— with,

make it through all— the rest— with, some - one I'll al -

McHALE'S NAVY MARCH

From the Television Series McHALE'S NAVY

Music by
AXEL STORDAHL

From the WARNER BROS. TV Show "THE DREW CAREY SHOW"

MOON OVER PARMA

(Main Title)

Words and Music by
ROBERT F. McGUIRE

Moon o-ver Par-ma, bring my love to me to-night..
Moon o-ver Par-ma, shine on I two seven-ty-one._

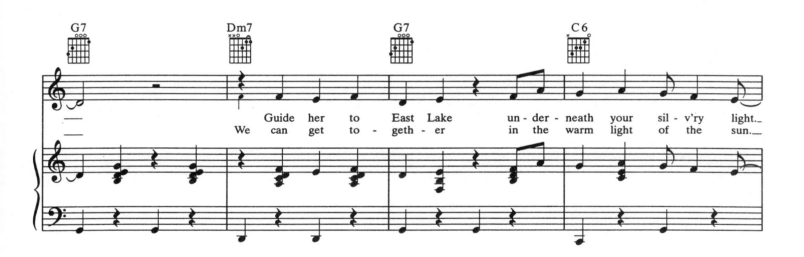

Guide her to East Lake un-der-neath your sil-v'ry light._
We can get to-geth-er in the warm light of the sun._

We met in Ash-ta-bu-la. She was do-in' the
I'm ask-in' you, don't fail. Get her safe-ly through

Moon Over Parma - 3 - 1

285

Main Title to the TV Show "THE JEFFERSONS"

MOVIN' ON UP

Words and Music by
JEFF BARRY and
JANET DUBOIS

Well, we're mov-in' on up to the east side to a de-luxe a-part-ment in the sky. Mov-in' on

Movin' on Up - 3 - 1

up   to the east_____ side.

We fin - 'ly   got   a   piece   of   the pie._

_____   Fish don't fry in the kitch - en;

beans don't burn on the   grill.   Took a - whole_ lot o' try - in'

MISTER ED

Words and Music by
JAY LIVINGSTON and RAY EVANS

A horse is a horse, of course, of course, and no one can talk to a horse, of course. That is, of course, un-less the horse is the fa-mous Mis-ter Ed. Go right to the source and ask the horse, he'll give you the an-swer that

Mister Ed - 3 - 1

From the TV Series "MURPHY BROWN"

MURPHY BROWN

Music by
STEVE DORFF

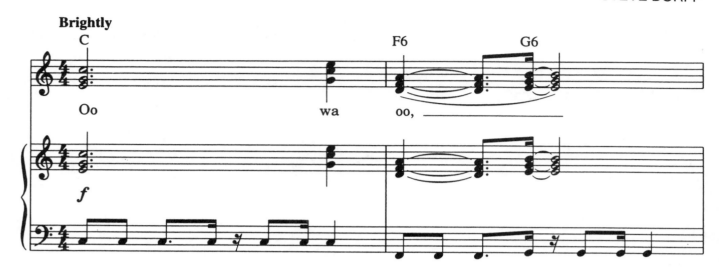

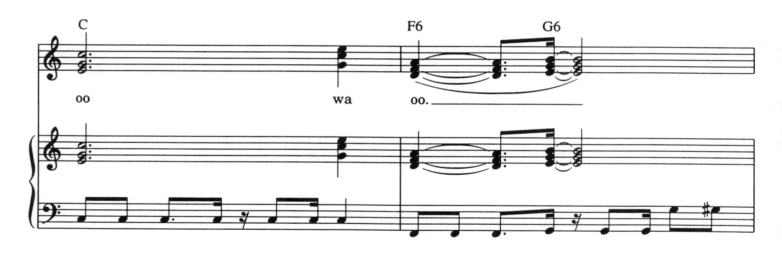

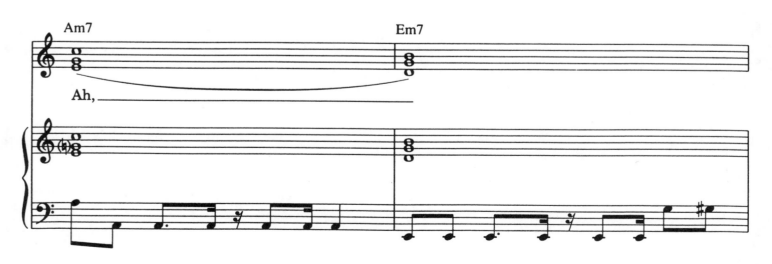

Murphy Brown - 2 - 1

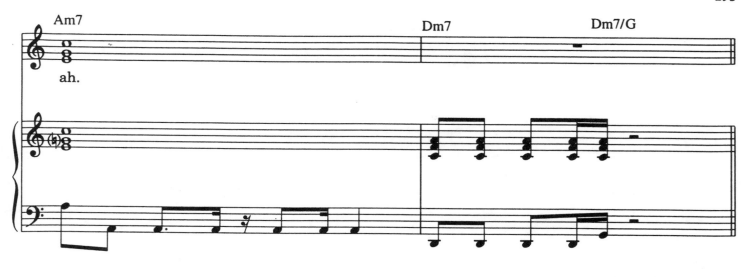

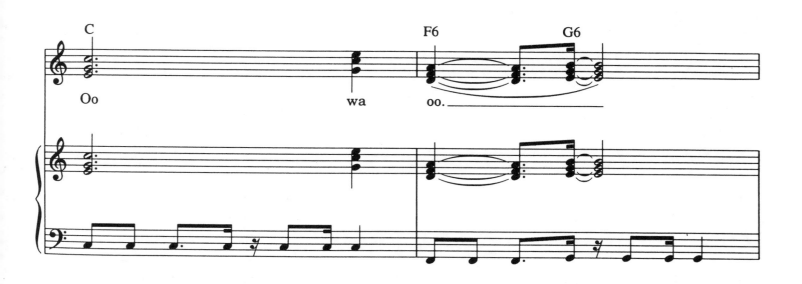

Theme From the TV Series "ONE DAY AT A TIME"

ONE DAY AT A TIME

Words and Music by
JEFF BARRY and NANCY BARRY

One Day at a Time - 2 - 1

SONG FROM "M*A*S*H"

(Suicide Is Painless)

Words and Music by
MIKE ALTMAN and JOHNNY MANDEL

Song From "M*A*S*H" - 2 - 1

1. Try to find a way to make
    All our little joys relate
    Without that ever-present hate
    But now I know that it's too late.
          And, Chorus

3. The game of life is hard to play,
    I'm going to lose it anyway,
    The losing card I'll someday lay,
    So this is all I have to say,
          That: Chorus

4. The only way to win, is cheat
    And lay it down before I'm beat,
    And to another give a seat
    For that's the only painless feat.
          'Cause: Chorus

5. The sword of time will pierce our skins,
    It doesn't hurt when it begins
    But as it works it's way on in,
    The pain grows stronger, watch it grin.
          For: Chorus

6. A brave man once requested me
    To answer questions that are key,
    Is it to be or not to be
    And I replied; "Oh, why ask me."
          'Cause: Chorus

Main Title From "HOPE & GLORIA"

THANK GOD FOR A FRIEND LIKE YOU

Words by
CHERI STEINKELLNER

Music by
CRAIG SAFAN

Thank God for a Friend Like You - 2 - 2

From the Twentieth Century-Fox Film "9 TO 5"

NINE TO FIVE

Words and Music by
DOLLY PARTON

Lively ♩= 104

mf

mf

Tum - ble out of bed and stum - ble to the kitch - en; pour my - self a cup
2. *(see additional lyrics)*

_ of am - bi - tion, and yawn, and stretch, and try to come_ to life._

Jump in the show - er, and the blood starts pump - ing;

Nine to Five - 3 - 1

301

Nine to Five - 3 - 2

302

Verse 2:
They let you dream just to watch them shatter;
You're just a step on the boss man's ladder,
But you've got dreams he'll never take away.
In the same boat with a lot of your friends;
Waitin' for the day your ship'll come in,
And the tide's gonna turn, and it's all gonna roll your way.
(To Chorus:)

Chorus 4 , 6:
Nine to five, they've got you where they want you;
There's a better life, and you dream about it, don't you?
It's a rich man's game, no matter what they call it;
And you spend your life putting money in his pocket.

Nine to Five - 3 - 3

Theme From the TV Show "ALL IN THE FAMILY"

THOSE WERE THE DAYS

Words by
LEE ADAMS

Music by
CHARLES STROUSE

Those Were the Days - 3 - 1

Those Were the Days - 3 - 3

THEME FROM "KEEPING UP APPEARANCES"

By NICK INGMAN

Theme from "Keeping Up Appearances" - 2 - 1

Theme from "Keeping Up Appearances" - 2 - 2

WKRP IN CINCINNATI
(Main Theme)

Lyrics by
HUGH WILSON

Music by
TOM WELLS

WKRP in Cincinnati - 2 - 1

As Performed by THE TORIES

TIME FOR YOU
(Main Title from "JESSE")

Words and Music by
STEVE BERTRAND, J.J. FARRIS
and MICHAEL SKLOFF

Tune guitar down 1/2 step:
⑥ = E♭ ③ = G♭
⑤ = A♭ ② = B♭
④ = D♭ ① = E♭

*E is enharmonic chord spelling of F♭.

Time for You - 3 - 1

true. Time to see_____ if there's a shoul-

der you_____ can lean_____ on._____ Time to be_____

_____ 'cause now it's time_____ for you._____

BEST FRIEND

Words and Music by
HARRY NILSSON

boy, cud-dl-y toy, my up, my down, my pride and joy.____

Verse 2:

2. Peo-ple, let me tell you 'bout him, he's so much fun,____ wheth-er we're

talk-ing man to man, or wheth-er we're talk-ing son to son. 'Cause he's my

best____ friend.____

Yeah, he's my

315

Best Friend - 3 - 3

HIGH UPON THIS LOVE
(Love Theme From "The Bold and the Beautiful")

Lyrics by DIONNE WARWICK,
ANDREW WEITZ and DAVID ELLIOT

Music by DAVID KURTZ,
JACK ALLOCCO and BRADLEY P. BELL

Slowly ♩ = 72

High Upon This Love - 5 - 1

318

High Upon This Love - 5 - 3

320

Verse 2:
They say love is truly blind,
And it will stand the test of time.
A love truly meant to be,
Two hearts as one so free.
I give my all.
You hold the key.
(To Chorus:)

Verse 3:
You are my shining light
In the shadow of the night.
It's the love that you see
In every part of me.
One touch, you set me free.

Verse 4:
Let's hold on to what we have,
'Cause love so often dies.
Won't be fooled by fantasy,
'Cause I believe in you and me,
And we'll never say goodbye.
(To Chorus:)

ALL FOR THE SAKE OF LOVE

Words and Music by
VICTORIA SHAW
and EARL ROSE

1. There's an an - gel ___ watch-ing o - ten -
2. I have dreamed ___ of ___ mo - ments ten -

From the CBS Television Series "AS THE WORLD TURNS"

EVERY BEAT OF MY HEART

Words and Music by
BRIAN McKNIGHT and EARL ROSE

Every Beat of My Heart - 6 - 1

From the TV Show "ANOTHER WORLD"

ANOTHER WORLD
(Theme)

By
JOHN LEFFLER and
RALPH SCHUCKETT

Another World - 3 - 1

Verse 2:
All my life I've been called a hopeless romantic,
Waiting for my prince to take me away.
But when I found you I felt different,
Than I've ever felt before.
Suddenly I was taking no chances
By walking through your door.
You are my . . .
(To Chorus:)

From the Television Show "GENERAL HOSPITAL"

FACES OF THE HEART

By DAVE KOZ,
JEFF KOZ and JACK URBONT

Faces of the Heart - 5 - 1

338

Faces of the Heart - 5 - 4

Faces of the Heart - 5 - 5

Theme From the PBS Television Series "MYSTERY"

MYSTERY

Music by
NORMAND ROGER

Mystery - 3 - 1

From the ABC Television Series "ALL MY CHILDREN"

I FOUND LOVE

By
PEABO BRYSON and EARL ROSE

Moderately, with feeling

Some will nev-er fall, and some will wait a

life - time.____ For that mo - ment, I would glad - ly risk it

I Found Love - 7 - 1

344

348

From the ABC Television Series "RYAN'S HOPE"

RIGHT FROM THE HEART

Words and Music by
EARL ROSE and
KATHY WAKEFIELD

Verse 2:

I loved you when there seemed no chance
That both of us could ever be together.
I love you now like I did then,
And when tomorrow comes I know that I will say
These words again:

(To Chorus:)

BONANZA

Words and Music by
LIVINGSTON and RAY EVANS

Bonanza - 3 - 1

354

Bonanza - 3 - 2

The *Ultimate* SHOWSTOPPERS *Series*

Movie

Piano/Vocal/Chords

More than 75 titles including: American Pie (from *The Next Best Thing*) • Change the World (from *Phenomenon*) • Over the Rainbow (from *The Wizard of Oz*) • The Pink Panther • Tears in Heaven (from *Rush*) • There You'll Be (from *Pearl Harbor*) • A View to a Kill • You Must Love Me (from *Evita*) and many more.

Television

Piano/Vocal/Chords

More than 115 TV titles including: Dharma and Greg • Every Beat of My Heart (from "As the World Turns") • The Pink Panther • The Power Puff Girls (End Theme) • Searchin' My Soul (from "Ally McBeal") • Sex and the City (Main Title Theme) • Theme from "Chicago Hope" • Theme from "Magnum P.I." • Theme from "The X-Files" • Walk with You (Theme from "Touched by an Angel") • Woke Up This Morning (from "The Sopranos") and many more.

Wedding

Piano/Vocal/Chords

More than 80 titles including: Evergreen (Love Theme from *A Star Is Born* • Forever I Do (The Wedding Song) • From This Moment On • I Do (Paul Brandt) • I Swear (All-4-One) • Let It Be Me (Je T' Appartiens) • Love Like Ours • This I Promise You • Tonight I Celebrate My Love • Two Hearts • The Vows Go Unbroken (Always True to You) • What a Difference You've Made in My Life • You're the Inspiration and many more.

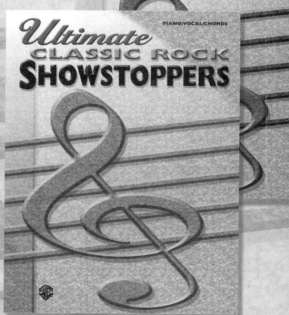

Classic Rock

Piano/Vocal/Chords

Includes: Against the Wind • American Pie • American Woman • Cat's in the Cradle • Don't Let the Sun Go Down on Me • Evil Ways • Hey Nineteen • House at Pooh Corner • Layla • Lyin' Eyes • Nights in White Satin and many more.

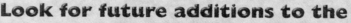

Look for future additions to the

Ultimate SHOWSTOPPERS *Series!*

AD1057 12/01